- P

This is not a self-help book filled with positivity and a feel-good message. There are plenty of books out there that will give you that. Rather, I've designed The Fear with the intention of producing results. The ideas and strategies found in this book are therefore intense and aimed at making you uncomfortable. Some of the practices that will be suggested are based on forcing you to experience emotional trauma. The process is completely self-monitored and regulated. With that said, if you have been clinically diagnosed with Post Traumatic Stress Disorder or Severe Anxiety please seek professional help before attempting The Fear. While these strategies can be extremely effective in producing results, the process is very precise and requires a degree of dedication and focus. Failure to correctly follow through with the process could produce poor results. The psychological risks will be addressed with every sensitive process suggested. Proceed with The Fear at your own risk, and be smart about your safety throughout this process. As I am not a licensed psychologist, take this as just my personal opinion on the process for mental change. The Fear is a psychological manual for mental change around anxiety and fear. Please study and understand the concepts and practices fully before attempting them.

THE FEAR

STRATEGIES FOR
FOR
SOCIAL ANXIETY
& OTHER FEARS THAT LIFE THROWS YOUR WAY

Justin Quinton

ISBN-13: 978-1511725392
ISBN-10: 1511725397

- Contents -

- Preface -

My initial goal in writing this was to compile the strategies and understandings that have helped me in my own life into a condensed step-by-step book. I originally wanted something I could refer back to just for myself. Because of this, you'll soon find that I write in a no-fluff, no-bullshit way that tries to get right to the point. The blunt, and at times, rather condescending writing is my attempt at trying to essentially bully myself into not being a little bitch when going through this process. Now if you're at all familiar with any personal development material, you'll probably appreciate the fact that I've cut out motivating stories and unnecessary babble just to entertain you. This is a very "cause-and-effect" style of writing, a straight meat-and-potatoes of making change and mastering over fear. It's a very tough-love, no-holds-barred approach.

I hope I get the pleasure of talking with you someday about your embarrassing moments, because believe me, I have plenty to share. As I've learned, social anxiety is something that can affect individuals differently. Sometimes it's general, sometimes it's just with girls or guys, and sometimes it's random. For myself in particular, it was with women. The moment there was any sort of flirtation or even just conversation with a girl I would get anxious to the point of puking. Gross, yes. Were there weird moments? Yes, but looking back now, they were hilarious. However, sticking true to the nature of this book, I'll save you the stories. But what I can say is that when I tell these stories to anyone who asks, it almost seems like I'm talking about a different person. These understandings and tools are life-changing, and I'm incredibility honored to have the opportunity to share them with you. I'm confident the ideas and concepts in *The Fear* will help you just as they've helped me. All the best with this journey, my friend.

- Instructions -

The Fear is broken down into seven stages. Each stage relies on the last so please do not skip ahead. This is a manual, to achieve optimal results take each stage one at a time. Read through the stage, and complete the challenges or assignments given to you before moving on. Once you feel confident that you have successfully applied or completed a stage, then move on to the next. Take this process seriously as the content is very condensed and needs to be understood. While you may be tempted to just skip the exercises and continue reading, please don't. Your success with this relies on your commitment to the process and its sensitivity. You should never try to attempt more than one stage a day. Even completing this in one week is being extremely ambitious. I've found this process works best for most people's lives when they take a month or two. But go at your own pace. This is about how you feel with each stage. So take your time, do the work, and get the results.

What would life be like if you could be your best self in any environment?

- Welcome to The Fear -

STAGE 1

- The Starting Point -

What is The Fear? The Fear is what I describe as the feeling that stops you from being social. It's the feeling that stops most people from approaching someone they find attractive, or striking up a conversation with a stranger. It's the anxiety that comes from public speaking, participating in class, or sharing your opinion in a meeting. It's the social inhibitions that people use alcohol or drugs to remove. It's a feeling of unease in social situations. It makes you over-think your actions. It puts you inside your own head, and keeps you from going after the things you want in life. Worst of all, it makes you uncomfortable with sharing your passions and creativity with the world. This fear, in essence, makes it impossible to be yourself, and to be confident when you need.

As a culture, we are facing a massive shift in the way people communicate. The majority of initial interactions with people don't happen face-to-face. They happen through social media, through messages, and behind the safety of a screen. You're more inclined to try to understand someone by analyzing their Facebook profile and pictures first instead of just talking to them. It's easier to live like this because you don't have to face The Fear. If you're a student, it is much easier to just go to your classes and then go home. And the same goes for work. But once at home, a lot of us then spend our time watching television or mindlessly scanning social media. The majority of people live their lives in this distraction, rather than challenge their fears or social inhibitions to make life juicy. This is where The Fear comes in. I've spent the last two years designing a process to push people past their social inhibitions and challenge them to question and conquer the fears that stop them from being their best selves.

Here's the truth: most of us have gotten into the habit of lying to ourselves about what's really stopping us when it comes to being social in real-life. It's not the lack of time, energy, or even the "know-how" that stops us. It's that we know damn well what's required emotionally, and we know that facing our fears is a tough business. A lot of us get in this habit of trying to make ourselves feel good in the moment, rather than face a problem. The warm glow of red as Netflix loads feels a whole lot better than the cold approach of the unpredictable. We know what we should do, but somewhere along the line, we have confused what we immediately want as the best thing for us. I want you to be honest with yourself: do you feel as though your social inhibitions are perhaps controlling you? Are you tired of the stress of being a social chameleon, or of dodging the idea that maybe, just maybe, you might have a bit more fun in life if you said yes to society? Do you feel like you are experiencing the best that a day can give you? My guess is no. The truth is most of us don't have what we want in life because we start believing the poor rationalizations that our brains make when we're scared.

Without getting too philosophical, René Descartes' statement "I think, therefore I am" is all we can truly know in terms of knowledge about life. Anything past this starts to get subjective. What that means to you as an individual, is that you can choose to interpret life as you please. You get to make up your own reasoning and your own mind about how your life is lived. Now you can choose to be a victim of circumstance or your past, this means spending your life reacting to the external world as it pushes you around and frightens you. You can also be the type of person who lets their fears dictate the type of people they meet and bring into their lives. And you can quickly let your fears stop you from sharing your creativity and individuality with the world. See, it's easy to just stay quiet, keep your head down, and wait for life to hand you things to "deal" or cope with until you die. Or you can get honest -- real honest -- and ask yourself if you're getting the most out of life. You can be the type of person that makes up their own mind about what they want and what they demands of life. You can be someone who doesn't just date whomever comes into their life, but rather has the courage to go introduce themselves to the people they want. You can be an individual who isn't afraid to speak up and share what they believe in. And most importantly, you can conquer your fears and start living on your own terms.

Most people will go through life on an automatic setting: they wake up, go to work, then fill up their free time with endless hours of digital distractions -- pretty much living on a rinse-repeat routine. They do the same things, they repeat the same patterns, and they come across the same problems in life. It's only when these problems can't be ignored that people stop distracting themselves and deal with life. Why is this? Because it's easy, it's comfortable and it requires no effort. It just means taking your attention away from your problems in life and vicariously living through the experiences of others. Now I know it can be pretty fun to sit back, judge, and critique, because at no point are you going to feel like facing failure. It's pointless to wait until you're motivated to face your fears. It's much more comfortable to ignore the fact that your getting fat rather than force your ass to the gym. It's easy to let life come to you, and to date the convenient choice or whoever chases you as opposed to forcing yourself to meet the people you want. The sad part is that it can actually seem more fun to just stay at home and binge-watch a television series instead of going out and socializing, but this is a lie you let your mind tell you. And most people will gladly accept this lie and live their lives like this. This world has no problem with you doing that either. Marketers and advertisers love to provide you with these endless opportunities to keep you distracted, because they know the truth: that most people just want to feel better, to feel good in the moment. They understand that most people just want to get back to doing nothing but being distracted. Comfort is addicting and very easy to sell. That is why people buy a product rather than dealing with their anxieties, but never end up using it. They purchase the product that promises good feelings, and the actual motivation to change disappears.

Just thinking they have the ability to change is enough to extinguish the actual desire to change.

Please don't let this be you. If you don't challenge yourself, if you don't become self-aware, your brain goes on that automatic setting. Tossing and turning with every moment, being motivated sometimes and sold another time, just repeating the same patterns. This automatic setting becomes active when you stop learning. When you don't face your fears, again the automatic setting gets turned on. This default automatic setting is serious business; it's just a reinforcement machine. It's a confirmation bias machine that continually provides its own evidence for what we can and can't do. At no point are you going to wake up one morning feeling ready for the challenges of life. That point doesn't come until you decide to face it. Until YOU make the decision and commitment to start facing your fears.

But here is what a lot of people don't understand. Your fears aren't staying dormant. Your anxieties aren't being cured because you no longer feel them in the moment. Just as you don't get ripped by purchasing p90x, your insecurities can't be a solved with a purchase. People's fears either grow or die, that's it. They're constantly changing and evolving with every experience you face. So every time you choose not to face your fears or choose to distract yourself, you've provided your brain with knowledge about that fear. You've given your brain evidence and a reference for how to handle that fear. Every time you want to speak up in class, approach a stranger, or share your creativity and don't because you were too afraid, you have given your brain another example of how your fear affects you. You have fed into the power of that fear. And the next time you're faced with it, your brain will look at all the other examples, and measure how intensely you should experience that fear. If you believe that your anxiety is going to get better later in life, without your effort, then you're lying to yourself. The time to master your fears, instead of them mastering you, is NOW.

So with that said, I'm not here to motivate you or to puff you up with silly affirmations or positive thinking. There are enough self-help products on the market that will do that for you. Rather, I'm going to push you. If you decide to continue, I'm going to make sure you are aware of your patterns and force you to be uncomfortable, as well as hopefully enlighten you on the psychology behind your fears and how they work. The truth about long-term development is that it comes from small efforts applied regularly to create powerful habits that then produce results in your life. I'm not interested in getting you temporarily hyped to have you feel like shit later because you still have the same results. Just like building your body up, it requires effort every day, but an effort you can add up to equal results. I want you to strengthen your psychology. This process is designed to get you to experience trauma in a strategic way that leads to powerful responses in your day-to-day life. There isn't a "magic pill" solution for results, otherwise everyone would have it.

There are a set of principles that consistently produce results. You can see these principles in anyone who has grown into a successful individual, either physically or mentally. It's the consistent ability to not settle for instant gratification, but to repeatedly experience the struggle of hard work or pain. It's making the shift, from being quickly appeased for a moment, to delaying your pleasure and reward until you've earned it. Just as there's a difference between reading a book and scanning the plot points, the people who spend the time to study a particular book carry a higher quality understanding of the book's meaning. They are able to consistently apply it to themselves throughout their lives, instead of just being aware of what the book was trying to portray. People who constantly work out and control their diet develop self-control and will-power that stays with them for life as opposed to those who opt to take drugs or develop eating disorders to control their weight. People who put in the time and effort on a consistent basis create habits and the focus to produce results. This ability is only earned, but once you get it, you keep that with you for life. This is seen all the time, because it applies to all other areas in life. People who have developed this ability to not quit when things get hard, whether that be in the gym, or school, or any of life's challenges, can usually succeed. It's not a matter of luck or of someone being "just the way they are". It's about strong psychologies and consistent effort. This ability stays with them for life so they are also able to succeed in areas like relationships or business. I'm not saying that all body builders will be successful in school or business. But I am saying they can be, if they choose to value those pursuits. People who can listen to their better selves and push though life's pains when their emotions tell them not to, earn their success. Another thing is that they aren't afraid to lose their success either. This is because they have developed the habits and built up mental road maps in their psychologies to take them back to success. In return, this allows them to take more risks, and produce greater and faster results in life.

2 TYPES OF PEOPLE

The bottom line is that there are two types of people. I call them the "I Am" people or the "I Can" people. The "I Can" people think they can do something but when opportunities arise for them to take action they don't. Whereas the "I Am" people are the type of people who do take action when the moment arises and who do produce results. There's a lot of things we "can do" in life. We can make more money, we can work out, we can handle our fears, but will we? Probably not, at least not until you become the person who puts in daily effort and hard work. It's not that most people don't want success. Most people just won't try for it, not because they don't want to be rich, or don't want to have their perfect body, or don't want to have their ideal mate, but because they haven't developed the discipline and habits beforehand to push through the pain and struggle that's required to get there. We are in an age of information, where figuring out the "how to do it" isn't the hard part. Yet most people believe it is, because they're used to the instant gratification of having things now as opposed to working hard for things worth having. I want you to change this for yourself. I want you to start to develop the mental habits to get what you want. Be the type of person who says "I am doing this" and not "I can do this".

My promise to you is that if you take this program seriously, do the work, and start to conquer your fears, you will experience a strength and confidence in yourself that no one can take from you. Trust me, you will enjoy life on your own terms, and you will feel an empowerment that can only be earned. You're never going to be without problems in life, and this can sound a little demotivating at first. But problems are just the indicators of how to better your life. It's human nature to have problems because that's your brain's way of showing you where you can grow. We all have problems, but the difference is in the quality of them. It's much better to have the problem of "which person is right for me" instead of "why doesn't anyone want to date me". The difference with the type of people who have higher quality problems is in their ability to face their fears. I want you to be able to have what you want in life. I want you to be able to have the confidence to share your talents and ideas with others, to date the people you want, and to have amazing relationships with people you choose because of compatibility rather than just circumstance. I want you to get the most out of life and to enjoy it rather than just cope with fears.

Throughout this program I am going to give you the strategies to not just handle your fears and anxieties in the moment, but to provide you with an understanding and game plan on how to master them. I'm not going to lie to you. I'm going to challenge you and push you past your comfort zone. I need you to commit to this. This starts with you demanding more of yourself, and from you wanting to control your life instead of it controlling you. This isn't magic or esoteric metaphysical crap; this is psychology. This is the science of understanding yourself and your demands for life.

It's time to start filling your life with the experiences that drive and excite you.

Please make the decision to commit right now. Take this seriously, and don't just let me make you feel good in this moment. Demand this of yourself.

CHALLENGE

This is your assignment for today: I need you to commit. Remember, this process is designed to challenge you and push you past your comfort levels. You WILL feel uncomfortable, but that's the point. If you do the challenges as they are assigned, you'll have no problem progressing through the tasks. This is designed to ensure your success.

I want you to sign or write a promise/contract to yourself, like "I, (your name), promise myself that I will commit to The Fear and complete the challenges to the best of my ability. This promise to myself is that I will demand a higher standard of life and not quit on myself throughout The Fear". If you think you could do better, write something that sounds significantly important in your own words. Sometimes these assignments might sound silly, and you'll feel stupid doing it, but just do it anyways. This is how progress is made, and it starts with you creating momentum daily. So right after you finish reading this stage, I want you to really start thinking about what it means to make a promise to yourself. What it would feel like to let yourself down? How would it would feel to not keep a promise to yourself? Spend a couple of minutes understanding what your word is worth to yourself. I know you might feel like joking around or not being genuine, but please take this seriously. Be fully aware that you will be challenged. It may be hard for you, and you will want to quit, but you are making the commitment now to the best version of yourself. Once this is clear, write down this promise. Or sign the contract on the next page. Once you do that, start Stage 2 tomorrow. Thank you for your commitment to the program and to yourself.

THE FEAR CONTRACT

I, _____,
promise myself that I will commit to The Fear
and complete the challenges to the best of my ability.
This promise to myself is that I will demand
a higher standard of life and not quit on myself
throughout The Fear.

_____   _____
Signature   Date

STAGE 2

- The What -

Before you begin reading make sure you have made the promise to yourself. If you want results with this program you'll need to get in the habit of fully and seriously finishing each stage before you continue on with the next. The challenges or exercises may seem simple or quick at times, so you might feel ok to move on without them or finish them later but for the sake of your progress make sure you do them before you continue. So If you have finished the first stage, congratulations for continuing, and making that commitment and dedication to yourself.

UNDERSTANDING FEAR
AND WHATS STOPPING YOU

Let's jump right into understanding the real reasons most people don't face their fears. Stage one briefly brought up the fact that most people live life on a default, automatic setting. In order to break this, you need a better understanding of what's going on underneath fear and how it affects you. With a better understanding, you will be able to start identifying fear from a new perspective, experiencing fear from a logical mindset rather than just being overwhelmed with the sensation of it. Knowledge about what's stopping you allows you to spot symptoms and stop automatic reactions. This awareness is the first part to conquering your fears.

WHAT STOPS US BIOLOGICALLY

The most important part of the human experience is our relationships with others. As humans, we are social creatures. Even if you're shy or consider yourself an introvert, we all still rely on human interaction for all sorts of things. Back in the Paleolithic Age, or "caveman times", we relied on others for survival; now it's for our mental well-being. Socializing is essential to our happiness and satisfaction in life. Things like romantic relationships, friendships and work culture make the largest impact on our day to day experience. It's the people we share life with that make it juicy, challenging and fun. Because of this our brains are hard-wired to be concerned for our reputation. Social activities like meeting new people, or introducing yourself to someone you find attractive, or more intensely, public speaking, can all threaten your reputation if things go bad. Back in our caveman times if you had a bad reputation, you were kicked out of the tribe. This meant certain death. So we've been wired to worry about the opinions of others, which to our brains seem like life or death. This is where things like stage fright, approach anxiety and even social anxiety come into play. Even though our caveman days are mostly behind us, it can still feel like the end of the world if you bomb a speech or embarrass yourself when meeting new people. But this old survival strategy no longer serves us like it did before. The problem is that we are a lot like old machines running extremely advanced software.

Our psychologies have evolved much faster than our bodies, because of how fast our societies have developed.

We aren't cavemen running away from lions anymore, but our bodies still can't tell the difference when we feel socially vulnerable.

So what happens when our bodies perceive danger? We go into what's known as the fight or flight response. Which means your body prepares itself to battle or run. Biologically, our bodies are wired to escape the perceived danger. Once you become aware of the social threat your hypothalamus, a part in your brain, tells your pituitary gland to secrete the hormone ACTH. This makes your adrenal glands shoot adrenaline into your blood. Your neck and back tense up, you start to slouch, and your legs and hands start to shake as your body essentially prepares for attack. You start to sweat, your heart starts to race, and your digestion system shuts down to better preserve energy to deliver nutrients and oxygen to your muscles and vital organs. This is also why you get butterflies in your stomach. Some people might vomit or feel nauseous, the intensity of the symptoms varies based on your genes, so don't take it personally if you're a puker. You are biologically wired to not experience social vulnerability. Your body uses this fight or flight response to get you to run from whatever the danger is or to attack it. To put this simply, you are hard wired to not rock to boat with other people.

WHAT'S THE MENTAL EXPERIENCE

As I'm sure you know, anxiety is much more than just a biological response. Our psychologies play into this fear as well, consciously and subconsciously. Logically, you know that if you just ran off stage, or started a conversation with a stranger and ran away, it would be just as bad if not worse socially then embarrassing yourself on the spot. So our psychologies have learned to step in before we experience that fear. They try to steer us away from situations like approaching someone or public speaking by making excuses or reasons for why we shouldn't do it to begin with. It's funny because the more intense the fear gets the more creative the excuses are. So when you try to reason your way into facing the fear you're really just fighting your imaginations ability to come up with why you shouldn't face the fear. An example of this would be wanting to approach someone you find attractive and then making assumptions about him or her like "oh, she's probably not single" or "he's busy and doesn't want to be bothered", or even denying and lying to yourself like "she's not that hot", or "I'm just here for the music", or whatever it may be. When we detect possible fear we rationalize; we come up with reasons as to why we shouldn't do something. It's the "I can do this, but" experience. Our psychologies love coming up with reasons about why we shouldn't do something. The reason it's so natural for us is because it's a psychological defense-mechanism that tries to keep us from experiencing the biological experience of fear. Just as your body automatically fights infection, your mind fights fear.

We have a fear of The Fear.

So when you're trying to convince yourself not to do something, your thoughts start screaming at you, and they'll try and psych you out if you'll listen. But say you push yourself past that. Say you act before you can think and you start experiencing the biological sensation of The Fear. You'll find that your thoughts actually speed up to an incomprehensible point. They become erratic and scattered to the point where the adrenaline kicks in and it diminishes your ability to listen or focus. You feel silenced, but not quiet. It's an inability to focus and choose your own thoughts. From this point, you're on whatever auto-pilot you have set in place as you experience The Fear. The psychological element that stops people from facing their fear is as much subconscious as it is conscious. Because this is the case, it's important to understand these auto-pilots and reactions in advance.

PSYCHOLOGICAL HOMEOSTASIS

So let's take a deeper look into what's going on behind the surface of what's stopping you from taking action.

It is my belief that we are hardwired biologically and conditioned psychologically to not push past The Fear. Now, before we get into tactics and strategies on how to get over The Fear, it requires an understanding of what's going on with us behind the curtains of our mind. I believe that people's refusal to take action to handle their fears comes down to what I call psychological homeostasis.

It sounds complicated, but it's really not. If you can remember from high school biology, homeostasis is just the process that maintains the stability of the human body's internal environment in response to changes in external conditions. Homeostasis is our self-regulator. It manages blood levels to make sure we maintain a pH level of 7.365. It makes sure we remain at the right body temperature. So if you get too hot you sweat, and if you get to cold you shiver. This is just the body's way of maintaining a "ready for anything" state. Well, I believe that a lot of the reason we don't take action, or rather, live passively with our fears instead of conquering them is because of a psychological homeostasis. It's the relationship between the brain's ability to produce the emotions we feel and our mind's ability to trigger them. It affects our motivation and actions, and our perception and experience. It explains a lot about why we do what we do, especially on the topic of fear.

Let's start by breaking down our emotions. Think of a spectrum from -10 to +10. This spectrum represents emotional intensity. All of the emotions you experience will live somewhere on the spectrum. But don't confuse good emotions as living on the positive side of the spectrum and bad emotions as living on the negative side. This spectrum is about intensity, so outward, motivating emotions live on the positive side and draining, energy-costing emotions on the negative side. If your energy and motivation was currency, emotions on the negative side would cost you money, while emotions on the positive side would give you money. So while emotions like joy or ecstasy live around a +9 or +10, so do emotions like rage and anger. The emotions that live on the positive side force action from you, and express behavior by themselves. So say you're in a good high-energy mood, you might just want to move around or "do something" with your friends. Or say you're out with friends at a club and you're just feeling fantastic, you'll find you're more in the mood to socialize or hit the dance floor. As your mood goes up, as the emotional intensity rises, you'll probably start getting louder and laughing more. It feels easier to move around and jump then it would in an emotionally-draining state. Think about being turned on, like really turned on, I'm talking real hot and bothered. That high sexual energy probably has you more fidgety or riled-up, and it becomes more difficult to stay still, right? This is because intense emotions create motion.

Let's even take a bad emotion, like frustration, for example. When you're frustrated at someone you might have a burning desire to give them a piece of your mind or voice how you feel. And if you're really angry, you might lash out physically and attack them. Intense emotions, good or bad, push you to take action.

So what about the negative side of the spectrum? These are emotions like exhaustion and nervousness or fear. Experiencing these emotions can drain you and make it very difficult to behave normally, or take any action at all. So the best way to categorize your emotions on this spectrum is to figure out if they force you to behave a certain way or cost you effort to behave a certain way.

So what now? Well, most people's brains are hardwired to live at 0 on the spectrum. Let's call this "home base" for now. Just like how our bodies are designed to survive and maintain the "ready for anything" state, our psychological states are the same way. This is where the term psychological homeostasis is coined from. Your brain is wired to always pull your emotions back to your "home base". Think of this as a protection strategy for your mind. It's trying to protect itself from psychological trauma and mental break-downs.

Allow me to explain: your mind is wired to remember emotionally-relevant events. Let me ask you a question: can you remember what color shirt you were wearing three Thanksgivings ago? Most likely not, this is because it's very difficult for people to remember small unimportant details like this, or what your day was like five years ago today, unless something relevant happened. The mind remembers things with emotional relevance and things that were emotionally intensive, like bad break-ups, public speaking, getting promotions, or any big life milestones. This is also how a lot of mental illness is caused. When soldiers experience traumatic events in war it's common for them to develop PTSD, because when people are forced outside of their spectrum of experience, they are at risk of psychological change. Depending upon the experience, that change can be good or bad. Your mind also remembers events where there are massive swings of emotion like going from embarrassment to anger or joy to exhaustion, so large emotional swings also put you at "risk".

So when you're forced to experience something anxiety-provoking that you've never experienced before and you have no idea what to expect, like public speaking or going to strike up a conversation with a stranger, your mind attributes the experience as -10 or worse. It knows you can't handle that fear with your current life experience, so it assumes you're extremely at risk of "mental damage", or in other terms, shifting your "home base". When bad things happen in your life or you go through some psychological pain, your "home base" shifts on the spectrum. Take a person who is dealing with depression, for example; their home base lives at a -2 or -3. Their psychological state is constantly being pulled towards an emotionally-costing and energy-draining state. In order for them to just feel nothing, let alone any positive emotions, they have to have things happen that bring them back to 0, and then above that. So say going to a party normally gives them a joy with an intensity of +4, well if their home base was at -3, going to this party is only bringing them to a +1. They're living in a constant state of effort just to function, additionally they are closer to the end of their negative spectrum which means, they're also less likely to survive any traumatic events that may come their way like losing a loved one or a job.

Our bodies and brains are designed to survive at all costs. This means we are supposed to be ready for whatever events come our way in life. The brain does this by releasing hormones that affect our emotional states, which change our thoughts and therefore our actions. Psychological homeostasis is the connection between the brain and the mind and how they work together to motivate us to take action or not. Our brains are wired to pull us back to our home bases where we are least at risk. Let me give you some examples of this. Imagine you work at some crappy retail job at the mall, so you have to fake a good mood or force acting professional. Acting this way costs you energy and effort. Let's say it pulls you to a -1 or -2. You can deal with it for now because you know work ends. Well, say you deal with a bunch of shitty customers, one right after the next. All of a sudden it's costing you a lot more to maintain that professional state and that fake good mood. So you're dropping down this spectrum and your emotional cost is now a -3 or -4 to pretend to be professional. Well now your brain is getting jumpy, so what happens is you start feeling frustrated, you start getting these bad, yet motivating emotions that push you in a different direction on the spectrum. This is your brain trying to pull you back to home base. It's trying to get you to stop faking the good mood by forcing your mind to get agitated enough so that you stop caring about behaving professionally. Or take, for example, being out with your friends, feeling fantastic, and having the time of your life. This joy is scoring around a positive 8 or 9. But what happens as it starts to get later in the night? Your brain starts to take you out of the moment and puts you in your head. You start to think about things more logically, your thoughts go towards all the things you have to get done tomorrow or things you have to deal with. Maybe you start to feel tired or exhausted, and "ready to go home". This experience is your brain pulling you back to "home base". Your brain can't justify the risk of this intensity much longer so the result is you having enough of living in the moment and partying for the night. Another example would be someone telling you some juicy gossip and asking you not to share it with anyone. But it's just so damn juicy that it's consuming all of your thoughts and focus. When things cost you energy, your brain starts to push itself back to 0 on the spectrum or "home base". So even though you were trying to keep it to yourself, maybe you just told some irrelevant person in a different social circle to appease the yearning sensation. Let me give you another example. Have you ever felt a massively overwhelming love for your boyfriend or girlfriend? Maybe you've felt so much passion for them in a moment that you've just needed to express it to them. But just as you try to hang out with them you find out they have to work or are busy with other things for the night. Well your brain tells your mind to miss them, and starts converting those intense outward expressive emotions into energy-costing and draining emotions to ease the passion and fire, leveling you at home base. Psychological homeostasis is the background explanation for our patterns and responses to life. Next time you feel a shift in emotions, try to fit them into this spectrum if you'd like a better understanding towards why you feel what you feel. This can also serve as a comforting thought for individuals who suffer from panic attacks or people who suffer from high self-monitoring, like those who repeatedly check their pulse. Knowing that your body and brain are designed to survive at all costs, physically and psychologically, can ease some thoughts. Psychological homeostasis will bring you back to home base automatically so just know any fear you experience will go away and is only temporary.

PSYCHOLOGICAL HOMEOSTASIS

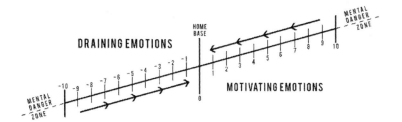

WHAT DOES THE EMOTION PROMOTE

NON ACTION	OR	ACTION
ANXIOUS		CONFIDENT
APPREHENSIVE		ANNOYED
FEARFUL		ANGRY
TERRIFIED		RAGEFUL
LONGING		PASSIONATE
RELAXED		EXCITED
TIRED		ENERGETIC
LETHARGIC		MOTIVATED
LAZY		INSPIRED
SADNESS		JOY
GRIEF		ECSTASY
DISINGENUOUS		AUTHENTIC
BORED		INTERESTED
EMBARRASSED		PROUD

CONCLUSION

So why is this important and where does social anxiety and fear come into this? Well, most people don't take action to conquer their fears because we are all hardwired to avoid danger and risk. Our bodies and minds will do whatever we can to avoid that fear of perceived possible death. Even when you have moments of motivation to get over the fear it can be extremely difficult to maintain that state, because your brain pulls your emotional state back to home base. Without knowing what's going on it's almost impossible to "will" yourself to actively want to experience the fear. That's why having this understanding of what's going on is essential to conquering The Fear. Your brain will not justify the risk and it will manipulate your emotions and thoughts to make sure you don't do it. So don't be so hard on yourself without knowing what's going on. If you have no experience approaching strangers or doing public speaking, and you're hardwired to experience fear when your reputation is at risk, then taking any action in the realm of social vulnerability exceeds your spectrum's thresh hold. Without the right strategies you're fighting a losing battle. If you don't have any memory references or experiences, you're not just fighting against stage-fright - you're also fighting the unknown. Your brain is imagining all of the possible things that could go wrong. It's a fight against your imagination and anything it can cook up. This is why most people won't face The Fear.

So before I go into how to combat this and before we look at strategies to handle The Fear, we need to engrave this understanding. I want to change your perspective on fear and anxiety. So start to see The Fear for what it actually is: an old, irrelevant, biological response that accidentally triggers when you want to have fun socially. Now, you may just be starting to face your fears or well on your way, and your genes may play into the way you experience The Fear's symptoms, but there are no excuses for not moving forward, so work with what you got and where you are. The only other choice is to play the victim in life, and miss out, which I can assume by the fact that you're reading this, is not what you want. So the first goal is to start to view this as just old-school caveman programming and realizing this in the moment. This is not actual death or anything to be worried about, but rather just hormones unnecessarily firing off. This is the first step to conquering The Fear.

Awareness and understanding while experiencing The Fear is the first step.

Without seeing it like this, your mind makes crazy associations and your fear grows. You want to be able to tell yourself in the moment that this is just a biological reaction. At first you won't believe it, and you might feel stupid telling yourself this, but once again remember the psychological homeostasis and its tricks. Once you do this, instead of you just blindly allowing your emotions and thoughts to push you into non-action or reaction, progress can be made.

CHALLENGE

So your goal in this stage is to identify and understand the sensation of The Fear as just a biological reaction once you're experiencing it. Don't worry about how to stop it or what you should do just yet. First get in the habit of seeing it for what it is. You need to start with a new perspective. Go out and test this; force The Fear to happen. Get in the habit of identifying the sensations as they happen. If you find someone attractive, entertain the idea of approaching them and starting a conversation. Notice how your body reacts to the idea, recognize how that sensation affects your thinking. Try to step away from letting it control you with automatic reactions and get in the habit of controlling your awareness when you face The Fear.

STAGE 3

- The How -

This stage focuses on some starting strategies on how to handle The Fear. While that may be tempting to just jump into, if you haven't finished the challenge of the last stage, make sure you do that first. Otherwise you're robbing yourself of possible progress. Don't just imagine yourself doing it. Actually go out and do it. This is an exact process that produces results, take your success seriously. If you have, then good work, and let's continue.

When dealing with anxieties of any kind there are two things that need to be managed. The first is the "in-the-moment response", which is The Fear that we talked about in stage 2. The second is the "long-term response", which is the anxiety. For clarity's sake, know that when I refer to The Fear I'm talking about the in-the-moment response, the biological response. And when I refer to the anxiety I'm referring to the long-term response, the psychological response. Both The Fear and the anxiety feed into each other. As you experience The Fear and don't face it, you fuel it and the anxiety, as well. As this feeling grows, The Fear response happens more easily and frequently. This goes on back and forth until a person develops a full-on social anxiety where just the thought of being social or just the thought of approaching a stranger triggers The Fear. So in order to work against this we need two continuous strategies. We need tools to handle The Fear in the moment and we need a game plan on how to progressively fight against the anxiety. We need both so that we can properly expose you to The Fear in a way that guarantees your success. When we do this we slowly deteriorate the anxiety. Simply put, the more you face your fears the less they affect you. The process of doing this is called exposure therapy or the really technical term in psychology is known as "systematic desensitization". But don't worry I'm not going to have you jump into anything you can't handle, but rather give you some small steps to help you desensitize.

Like I explained in the last stage, a lot of what makes fears difficult to face and why people don't take action comes down to the psychological homeostasis. When you're feeling neutral or at your emotional home base of 0, the thought of going up and approaching a stranger or introducing yourself to that person you've been crushing on can be seen as too much of a emotional risk. Especially if doing that is not something you're used to. You could embarrass yourself, or not know what to say, or freeze up once you started. When you don't have much experience with something like this, your brain has no reference point. It has no experiences to size this up against. So what happens? It defaults the experience at a -10, pretty much resulting in you not doing anything but dodging the situation or believing the excuse as to why you can't take action. Well, let's look a little more into the daring activity, shall we? How do you behave when you've had a few drinks in you? How easy is it to be social when you're in a great mood? Think about going on a date with someone and how maybe it was hard to make conversation throughout the date. But right when the night is ending and you have to go, conversation suddenly picks up as you're about to split ways. What's going on here is that as the tension gets higher, and as the time becomes limited, your emotions spike. It's like when you've been drinking and partying and your emotions are high, and your social inhibitions are low, you probably have no problem approaching a stranger or doing things that (putting it nicely here) you might question when sober. Even just being in a good mood for whatever reason will make it easier and even more enjoyable to have a conversation. You've probably found you're more daring with your humor, like having no problem being crude or sharing more personal information then you would in a neutral mood. When our emotional state is raised on the positive side of the spectrum our bravery raises and social inhibitions and anxieties drop.

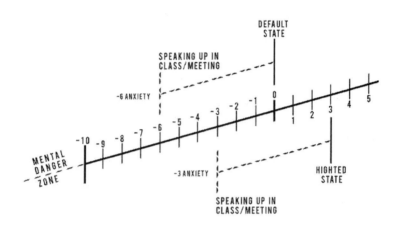

It's all about momentum. It's like being on a roll - things just flow, you can be your best self. Have you ever been on a roll in conversation and said something that was very cool or witty? Then after you thought to yourself, "I can't believe how smooth I was. I'm never that cool". Momentum pulls out our best selves. The same works for bad emotions, however. When we feel angry, we can say things and do things that we might not do in a calmer head space. This is how you want to first approach your fears.

You need to be in a heightened emotional state, so put yourself into a good mood.

Do whatever you need to in order to boost your emotions before you challenge yourself. A lot of people end up psyching themselves out if they know they're actively going out to face a fear or complete a challenge I give them. So what you can do instead is next time you're naturally in a good mood, do the challenge! It's much more fun to handle your fears like this instead of using high emotions like anger to drive you to action. But there is no doubt that those emotions can work too. Individuals who are crazy and demand results quickly and can handle rough emotions will also take advantage of the dark side. So if you start getting angry at yourself because you feel like chickening out, that self-anger can often feel worse than the anxiety of actually facing The Fear, and force you into action. Using anger is pretty extreme and can go bad so I would recommend sticking to your good emotions to drive you at first. What you're aiming for is momentum, and getting yourself "on a roll". It can be very overwhelming to approach the hottie at the club the moment you walk in. So start by talking to people you don't find attractive. Get in the momentum of regular conversation. If this is too much start by making little complements to passing people. If this is still too much, ask for the time or where the bathrooms are or any other basic question. You need to start the momentum and start at a place where you can progressively succeed.

Because everyone has different levels of anxiety, and different scenarios and triggers, you need to set up the right steps for yourself. You do this by pushing on your fears, gauge what causes you to take non-action and fill in steps that lead up to that action. If you're a student with social anxiety start by hanging around the school more, don't just run home after class. Try just making little comments to people or by asking basic questions. Then start introducing yourself to the person sitting next to you in class or just making any comment or question about the teacher to the person like "have you ever had this prof before?" Then start by trying to answer or ask a question in class. Start by trying to make just one comment per class, or one per day, depending on where you're at. You want to keep upping the intensity and weight but start from a manageable place. The best part about this process is the adrenaline and hype you get after you push yourself. As you start to do this, don't worry about the results of what was said or how you came across. Just focus on completing your challenge and enjoy the hype after.

Start building a momentum with facing your fears, step by step, progressively giving your brain new references and experiences on how to handle fear and your response to it.

Two things are going on here: the first is that the "in-the-moment" fear becomes desensitized. It can very quickly get to a point where you have zero fear about things that used to absolutely paralyze you hours ago. I see this all the time with people who start approaching women at the club. Once the momentum is built, it's tough to stop them. Once they feel confident and get the ball rolling, they just want more challenges and goals. The sad truth behind this is that for a lot of people, this is the first time they have felt confident and in control to be their best self. The process is incredibly empowering and addictive. The second thing that happens when you face your fears with momentum is its effect on the long-term anxiety. The anxiety starts to break down because you're adding more evidence for your brain that this is an unnecessary response. As this happens it learns that it can reserve its energy for other things, rather than just wasting it on worrying and trying to protect you. It's the equivalent of your brain finally accepting that you're an adult now and don't need to be babied, and that it doesn't have to warn you of danger.

The truth is, the anxiety was created because of not taking action, and that non-action was the result of you buying into your imagination's ability to manufacture any bad possibility.

This is why trying to analyze your anxieties is like fighting a losing battle. You're fighting against all the possible things to be afraid of. You're fighting against the unknown. So trying to logically talk yourself through your anxieties is like fighting your own imagination; it never ends. This is why we need to face our fears up front. It's about attacking the anxiety at its roots verses fighting every branch. As you start to do this more, things like public speaking and approaching the babe no longer seem like -10 but rather -9 or -8. As you start to break the anxiety, the fear doesn't trigger as intensely or as easily. The once unknown fear of your imagination is starting to become known. What's really going on is that you're starting to get new references of being socially vulnerable and surviving. So while this can still be scary, facing the challenges are manageable in the right emotional state. Think of this as chipping away at the ice sculpture of the unknown.

Now this process isn't rocket science. It's actually

incredibly basic and simple, but don't confuse this for being easy. Here's the thing: The Fear is constantly growing or dying as you handle it in every moment. Even with creating that progressive momentum in the moment and in life, The Fear will always be there. The difference will be how it affects you and your thoughts. Even the most experienced public speakers and performers still get nervous before going out on stage. But the difference is that the sensation of The Fear actually juices them. It helps them to get in the state rather than inhibits them. The Fear is something that can massively help you once you re-learn and re-associate its meaning.

Now, so far all of this has relied on your ability to push yourself, and take action to experience manageable fear. And while this is good, the process can take a while. Depending on the level of your fears and anxieties as well as your personal commitment and bravery, the speed of your results may vary. This could be a power-house week of fear-facing if you're crazy and driven. Or it could be months of progressive development.

EXTERNALIZING CONTROL

If you want to really super charge your results, here is a psychological strategy that can help speed up the process and motivate you to create momentum. It's called Externalizing Control. Essentially, you want to let your logical mind force you into situations and pay the emotional cost later. This is done by committing to something that you can't back away from. Simply put, you can remove the possibility to chicken out or be a little bitch. An example of this is committing to do public speaking, like saying you will MC a wedding of a friend or give a toast. Or you join a club or group at school, or sign up for a party committee at work. Or maybe you join a play or take an improv class. This is you getting into the habit of listening to your logic verses your emotions. It's planning with a reason-based head and paying the emotional cost later. This is how progress is made in psychology, when you start to control your emotions verses them controlling you. If approaching women at the club freaks you out, externalize the control. Plan to go out with a friend, tell them to force you to approach and to not allow you to bail on the plans. Give someone else the power to over-ride your irrational emotions. If money motivates you, give your friend $100 in fives and have them give you back a fiver for every time you talk to someone. Make not facing your fears more painful than just disappointing yourself. It's one thing to disappoint yourself or lie to yourself but it's something completely different to fail a friend or to not follow through with a commitment when other people are involved. Again, see this as a small step. It's not you signing up for weeks of hell and worry, but just saying to a friend that you will do something. Keep your focus on the action at hand, not on what you'll have to go through to complete the challenge. Whenever you're facing your fears, it's always better to see the process in stages and challenges. Then just baby-step your way there, or leap if you're crazy. If you focus on the whole picture of it, you won't do it. So keep your focus on the moment at hand and the end goal only. Anyone who has gotten into working out or exercise knows that it's much easier to get started if you have a gym partner. When you externalize control, you allow yourself to be motivated by others, rather than just yourself. Have your friends be teammates or coaches who can help push you. It makes the process way easier than trying to manage your own emotions and discipline and focus all at once. This will also drastically improve your results by turning the process of conquering The Fear into an "I have to" instead of an "I should".

So to summarize everything, we need to face our fears head-on in order to get over them. This is done by forcing ourselves to be socially vulnerable. The strategies that can be used to fight against our psychological homeostasis are:

First: Be in a heightened state. The more intense your emotions are the easier it will be for your brain to justify the psychological risk or cost.

Second: Build a momentum. Take this step-by-step, and progressively work up to the harder challenges to ensure success.

Thirdly: Externalize control to help you get results quicker and to maximize your motivation.

Because the in-the-moment biological response of fear and the psychological long-term anxiety are so interconnected, it's important to use these tools together to ensure your success.

CHALLENGE

I want you to think about some immediate actions you can take to externalize your control. What can you commit to doing that would push you? Decide this for yourself now and right as this stage ends take immediate action to plan to do it. Don't wait, do it right as you're done with this stage, whatever it may be. Commit to doing something with people and with your logical state plan to be socially vulnerable in the future. Sign up for some volunteering, put yourself in a group environment, join an improv club, or call your friend to go out or ask them to push you to go and introduce yourself to whomever the crush is for you. I know it's easy to just read this and to move on to the next stage but please do this for yourself. Even if it's small, pick something, pick anything. You made a promise to yourself, it's time to keep it.

What would push you past your comfort zone?

_____

How could you set yourself up to do that?

_____

Who will hold you accountable for this?

_____

When will you take action to make this happen?

_____

And just when you thought this stage was done, I have one last thing I want you to start doing. I will explain the importance of this more in detail later. For now I want to get you started on building momentum.

Have a staring contest with the strangers you pass by on your way to school or work or whenever you are in public.

As you pass by strangers going the opposite way, make eye contact with them and don't break it until they do. Every time they look away that counts as a win. Every time the anxiety gets to you and you look away, you lose a point. Try and get 10 points a day at least. And if you get into any trouble, just apologize and say you spaced out or you thought you knew them or just wish them a nice day. This can be extremely anxiety-provoking but this is an easy way to build up some momentum. I'll explain more about why I'm having you do this later. But for now go externalize control and commit to being socially vulnerable, and go full creeper by winning some staring contests. Good luck, friend.

STAGE 4

- You Vs. Yourself -

Before we begin this stage, please make sure you have completed and applied the principles and challenges of the last stage. I can offer you some tools and new perspectives on anxiety but ultimately until you get out into the field you're never going to feel the change and get success with this process. So if you're following along and completing the challenges, congratulations and welcome to Stage 4. This stage is split into two parts because I've found most people have thresholds on how many new concepts they can take in at one time. Please take your time absorbing this information. Like everything so far, it requires the understanding of prior stages. If you need to break this stage into multiple days, please do so. You're better off having lasting success from a quality understanding over short term, quick results.

PERSONAL CHANGE

I am a big believer that people are able to change parts of themselves once they become educated on what that part is. My philosophy on personal change looks like this, it begins with the motivation to change. Then that motivation pushes a person to educate themselves on the issue and how it affects them. When the person knows what's going on and understands how they normally react, they get what I call "awareness".

Awareness gives the individual a choice; it allows the person to step away from the automatic response or behavior and choose to react differently. As the person starts to respond differently they start to make new associations on how to automatically respond.

It's a process of conditioning. Simply put, it goes "why should I change" to "what should I change" to "how should I change". Stage 1 of this program focused on the "Why" you should get over fear. Stage 2 focused on the "What" is stopping you from taking action. Then Stage 3 focused on the "How" to get over the fear. Now that we have the basics down, we are going to step it up a notch with each stage as we get into the more advanced part of this process that deals with the particulars. Stage 4 will deal with how The Fear affects your confidence, which is your relationship with yourself.

CONFIDENCE

Now you've probably heard "confidence is everything", and that's not completely wrong. Confidence is a cognitive trait that demonstrates a high self-esteem and self-worth. It shows the comfort you have with yourself. Socially speaking, confidence is the opposite of anxiousness. Anxiety makes it impossible for you to be yourself with others. Maybe you've had the unfortunate experience of finally working up the courage to go talk to the "Hot Flash" in your class or the "10" at the bar and not being able to think of anything to say. Perhaps you found yourself monitoring and filtering what you said to them, or trying to alter your natural behavior when around them. This is the result of anxiety, and a lack of confidence in who you are. Think about when you're with your family or friends, you probably have no problem keeping up conversation or talking freely. This is because you know they've accepted who you are, and there's a confidence and comfort in that. So once you accept who you are, that same comfort follows you in all scenarios. When this happens you'll have no problem coming up with things to say when you need to make conversation.

So in summery, confidence allows you to feel at ease

with being yourself in a social experience. It's this lack of confidence or anxiety that prevents you from speaking up or participating in something you know you're good at.

Confidence is attractive to both sexes, and people are naturally drawn towards it. This is because when you have it, you demonstrate a ease with yourself that makes people feel like they can trust you. It also feeds into itself, as people want to be around you more, you feel more accepted. The more acceptance you feel on a regular basis, the more self-love and self-worth you'll have, meaning more confidence.

When you're feeling confident you're not feeling anxious.

Confidence is also the behavioral demonstration of competency. This is why a lot of people only feel confident in their area of expertise, which isn't a bad thing. It's perfectly fine to not feel confident about things you know nothing about. In fact, admitting you don't know something can also demonstrate confidence at times. But the confidence being talked about now is about the state of being ok with yourself, and knowing your own value in any social situation.

But with all that said, I'm not going to leave you high and dry by telling you to "just be confident". Real core confidence is something that's conditioned in. Anyone can get themselves puffed-up and cocky in the moment. But what I'm talking about is a genuinely developed foundation of ease, a real comfort with who you are. This genuine ease and confidence is something that radiates from you on a daily basis. Stage 4 will give you the tools to psychologically engineer yourself to have this confidence.

THE ORIGINS OF CONFIDENCE

Confidence essentially comes from our feelings about who we are. If you feel good about who you are, you radiate confidence, and if you feel negatively about who you are, you don't. It's the evaluations of what psychologists call our self-concepts. It's these self-concepts that make up our identity. So what is a self-concept? Well, it may be as simple as a phrase such as "I'm funny" or "I'm smart". Or it could be more complex, like a particular belief or value like "I'm an Agnostic", or "I'm a person who values hard work". We also form self-concepts around objects or achievements like "I'm the fastest runner in my school". The purpose of these self-concepts is that they allow us to identify with the external world, such as people, experiences, or things. An example of this would be seeing a t-shirt or car and deciding "that's not me". Or even with our challenges like winning staring contests or asking for phone numbers and thinking "I'm not the type of person to do that". Our self-concepts play a massive role in how we interact and perceive the world. This is where anxiety comes in. So you've heard me reference a lot about "teaching your brain how to react" or "conditioning the new response". Well, this is what I was referring to. What we are doing when we face our fears is teaching our brain new self-concepts. It's teaching new ways on how to respond to situations that provoke the fear.

SELF CONCEPTS AND ANXIETY

A lot of people hold self-concepts like "I'm just socially awkward" or "I'm just shy". It's self-concepts like these that hold people back from attempting to change. As you start to challenge and fight against these self-concepts you'll not only experience The Fear response, but an identity discomfort. It's an awkward in-your-skin feeling at first. Please keep this in mind throughout the process. These self-concepts that make up "who we are" also tell us how to react. They are conditioned in us by previous experiences. They are the excuses and lies we tell ourselves to try and avoid situations that make us feel The Fear. I'm sure you've connected the dots if you've been following along. When I talk about most people being on an automatic setting in life or how your anxieties are continually growing, I'm talking about the self-concepts. It's the self-concepts that are making up your social anxieties. This is because they cause you to compare and relate yourself to the external world. As you encounter new experiences and people, you are faced with how to relate and react to them. So for a socially-anxious individual, that usually results in avoidance reactions. These are the thoughts like, "she's not that hot", or "he's probably not my type" that try to trick you into not following through with being socially vulnerable.

Part of the anxiety is triggered when you take action against your self-concepts by facing your fears. You're losing who you think you are. You're losing part of your identity. This can feel like a massive discomfort in your own skin at first.

But at some point in your life, you need to draw a line in the sand and decide which parts of your identity are serving you and what parts aren't.

If your beliefs about yourself don't bring you closer to your true wants, you owe it to yourself to reject those negative beliefs. So in terms of anxiety, its time to trim the mental fat. But because these self-concepts are your way of responding and relating to life, good chance they are the product of you trying to avoid The Fear response. They are there to essentially protect you from perceived harm. This is the made up rationalizations your mind makes to convince you into not taking action. So to your brain, this is you breaking down your mental defensive system. But you should logically know better by now to ignore that.

So as you start to approach the hottie or force yourself to be more social, you start to break down self concepts like "I'm shy" or "I'm socially awkward". Once this happens, your brain starts supporting new self concepts like "I'm a sociable person" or "I'm a great public speaker". Just remember that shifting your identity can feel uncomfortable at first. So see The Fear response as the pain you get while working out. That burn you feel is good, it means you're getting some serious gains. The Fear is no different.

THE NATURE OF SELF CONCEPTS

With an understanding of how self-concepts develop and function, you can also understand why your anxieties and fears grow. The reason behind this constant growth is because our psychologies are designed to protect us, just as our bodies are.

For the same reason that our body builds up our immune system, the mind constantly builds up its own defense system. This process is done by continuously looking for ways to re-enforce and re-support your self-concepts. It does this by automatically perceiving experiences in a way that serves as evidence for your current self-concepts. Like looking through a particular lens at an experience, it only picks up on the details that it needs for support. So let's use a person who identifies with being socially-awkward, for example. That person will perceive a regular interaction in a socially-awkward way. This person will take an interaction that most people would consider normal and hyper analyze it to the point of making it a socially-awkward experience. Its purposely placing an attention to insignificant details that would otherwise go unnoticed. When this is done, the experience is taken as evidence or support for the socially-awkward self-concept.

Have you ever had the experience of misinterpreting a text message from someone as being extra sassy or negative, only to find out that they didn't mean for it to be taken that way? This is exactly how your identity and its self-concepts can incorrectly interpret things. Or imagine having self-concepts like "I'm not attractive" or "I'm ugly". Your mind will start finding evidence to support those.

You will start to spot flaws in your appearance that no one else would have even noticed. You will start to compare yourself with all the attractive people you pass by, completely ignoring all the people you'd rate yourself more attractive than. Even worse than this, a lot of people will go out of their way to support a self-concept. They might only pursue people they know will reject them. Just so they can have the reassurance of "see, I told you, I'm just ugly" victim mentality. Rest assured that when our identities are involved, so are our egos. This is also how a lot of self-fulfilling prophecies come into play. As we provide our own supporting evidence, we create our own perceptions. The psychological term for this is called the confirmation bias. We even use others to support our identities. An example of this is having a self-concept like, "I have good taste in music" and then only showing music to friends who share the same music tastes as you. We think things are "matter-of-fact", or "just the way things are" because we have evidence to prove it. But this evidence is self made, and it's important to remember this. Now, I'm not saying that all of our self-concepts are bogus, but rather, that a lot of what we identify with is self-confirmed.

We are hardly in the business of perceiving things accurately. Especially when our self-concepts are often the result of trying to avoid an imagined fear.

Try and find flaws or gaps in your own identity, how do you really know who you are? Try and poke holes in the elements and beliefs about yourself that don't serve you. While it may make be uncomfortable to question yourself, it is also very freeing. Once you understand that "who you are" is the product of your decisions, you will have a level of control over your life that most people never bother to achieve. But this introspection can be tricky at first, especially once you start to face your anxieties and fears. Just watch how your thoughts try to trick you as you start facing your fears. Let's take our approaching the eye candy at the club example. Once you do it, and survive (maybe you just embarrassed yourself a little), your mind has to make sense of the fact that your body unnecessarily released a surge of adrenaline. So while you're feeling on top of the world and hyped up because you survived, there's a bit of an internal dialogue going on with your brain and your mind. As explained before, the way your mind perceives the experience and how your brain perceives social vulnerability is very different. The dialogue being had with your self talk might sound a lot like: "Woah there psycho! Do you have any idea on how lucky you are to have made it out alive? Believe me, that won't be the case next time. So cut the shit, and don't pull a stunt like that again, you hear me? But, umm, good work". Then after the next approach that night, your brain pipes up again with the feeling of adrenaline: "Alright you fucking daredevil, what are you, a bloody glutton for punishment? You a big hot-shot now, hmm? God damn that was close! Fun, sure, but way too risky. Let's tone'er down a notch, ok?" Say you keep pushing yourself and you keep talking to people throughout the night. As you build up that momentum, this internal dialogue eventually turns into "This is mission control, we see the vixen to your 9 o'clock. You are clear to approach. (Radio out static). Roger that, I'm approaching the target". To stay the least, there's a massive shift in your internal dialogue. But what's really going on is your self-concepts are changing, and this is resulting in a new way to react to these situations. You'll be amazed on how quickly life long fears can disintegrate within a night.

Just like working out, it's a lot easier to maintain muscle than to build it. Or to maintain your weight, rather than loosing it. As the new self-concepts settle in, you can relax your efforts. Once you settle into being the type of person who can approach strangers, and who can be themselves around new people, you won't have to go through these massively anxiety-provoking experiences every chance you get. Mainly because anxiety no longer holds power over who you are anymore.

- Stage 4.5 -

So with an understanding of self-concepts under our belt, let's get back to confidence. Like I said earlier, confidence comes from how we feel about our self-concepts or "who we are". If you evaluate your self-concepts as positive and helpful to your life, you feel better about yourself and your identity. This results in more self-esteem and more confidence. The opposite is true if you don't.

The question now becomes, where do we go from here? Well, there are two strategies. The first is to take advantage of your brain's ability to believe whatever evidence you feed it. Your brain does this automatically. So instead of trying to slowly break down and analyze all of our complex identities to see if they're valid, we're better off to go with the natural ability and motion of how self-concepts are made and essentially "write over" the old ones.

ADJUSTING YOUR R.A.S.

The process of "writing over" our self-concepts is done by adjusting our Reticular Activating System, or R.A.S. for short. The R.A.S. is primarily used to transition a person from sleep to wakefulness and vice versa by adjusting our alertness. But it's also responsible for what our brains place attention to, or becomes alert of. This component in the brain helps sort out what's relevant or important to us, so we can gain more evidence for our self-concepts.

An example of the R.A.S. in action would be having a friend showing off their new Mini Cooper, and then starting to notice Mini Coopers everywhere for the next week. In this example, it's important to remember that the Mini Coopers were always there, it's just that your brain didn't pick them out until they were brought to your attention. So if we want to support new self-concepts we need to adjust our R.A.S. to notice new evidence. This is done by forcing our minds to focus on the evidence we want. We need to repeatedly and constantly do this until our brain gets in the habit of doing it automatically. In the example of the Mini Cooper, it stands out because there's probably nothing contradicting its ability to stand out. But when it comes to our self-concepts we need to work against the negative ones already in place. This is why it's necessary to force your focus, while exaggerating the positive evidence.

Start by looking for what makes you downright sexy. Start answering the question of "what makes you so irresistible to others?" Look at yourself in the mirror and superficially love every part of you. Start by noticing your best features, see them as absolutely flawless, like they were crafted out of marble. Then look at your worst features and sell them to yourself. Actually talk to yourself out loud - you're not overweight, you're voluptuous or curvy. Find your own evidence for why you're so fantastic. If you're bald, start to see yourself as a bad-ass bald guy like Jason Statham. See even your worst flaws as just elements that "even the playing field" for everyone else because you're just so damn attractive. Force yourself to be narcissistic, superficial, and egotistical when you talk to yourself or see yourself in the mirror. Have fun with this; don't take yourself so seriously. Don't be afraid of working your way over towards your personality as well. Stroke your ego by complementing your favorite cognitive traits. Continue doing this until you no longer need to force it, and it no longer feels silly.

I know this may seem like a stupid process that just trains you to be a cocky asshole, but stick with me here. I'm assuming you have grown up in a westernized culture. So without straying too far off topic, you've grown up in a society with a very heavy focus on marketing and advertising. The way advertisers motivate people to buy things is by playing on our insecurities. They sell to our insecurities by showing us images of people having what we want. They never mention your insecurity so you don't get defensive, but rather show you ideals in life that have you comparing yourself. They then place a product in-between what we are insecure about, and the people who appear to have what we want. The funny thing is the "solution" they're providing is often gimmicky or completely unrelated. But because of the associations and the power of our insecurities, we feel motivated to purchase. Take for example all of the "get abs" exercise products available. They show you images of these ridiculously cut individuals with not just massively defined abs, but muscular arms and bodies. Well I can promise you those models didn't get there by the exclusive use of that product. Logically, people know this but when their insecurities get into the picture, it's game over. They're a believer and excited to "buy" their abs. There is a science to getting you to purchase products, and companies pay large amounts of money to play on our psychologies. But the point I'm making is that every time this happens we are fed a little shred of "evidence" that we aren't enough. Or that without this or that product we aren't attractive or stylish. The average person is exposed to 3000 or more advertisements a day.

Now while you're not actively focusing on all of them, your subconscious is. So take into account that your brain is automatically searching for ways to get more support for your self-concepts. And you can imagine the powerful influence advertising has on how we feel about ourselves.

The good news is that a purposeful and conscious focus of your attention carries way more power over your self-concepts than any automatically added evidence.

So when you start to purposefully "sell yourself" to yourself, you start to create powerful evidence very quickly. I know you probably feel ridiculous with just the thought of doing this. And at first it's just going to feel like you're lying to yourself. But those contradicting thoughts of "oh shut up and stop lying to yourself", or "who are you trying to convince here?" are just the products of poor self-concepts trying to resist contradicting evidence. Eventually, as you continually give your brain more reasons than not when thinking you're sexy, it starts to believe it. Your brain doesn't care if it's a lie or not. Now, your existing self-concepts on the other hand might try to call you out on it at first, making you feel stupid for even trying this. But eventually you'll start to believe the new evidence and those thoughts stop. This is where this process of adjusting your R.A.S. gets extremely clever. Even though you logically know you're not the sexiest person on this plant, your brain doesn't. So as you start to grow these cocky self-concepts, your behavior and automatic thinking will start to shift. You will start to interpret experiences very differently. For example, if you catch someone looking at you, your first thought becomes "oh they must be checking me out", whereas before this process, it might have been "do I have something on me, or is my hair a mess, or do I look bad?". Another example is if you try to strike up a conversation with someone you find attractive, and they respond rudely or cold, your first thought becomes "someone's having a bad day" or "well, someone's a douche" as opposed to "Oh fuck, I just embarrassed myself! Oh god, this is awkward. I knew I shouldn't have bothered them". On top of all this, confidence is a cognitive trait that people pick up on. It's not a physical feature. So as you start to buy into your own evidence, you also change the impression you put out to people. We are all practical psychologists that are wired to pick up on the emotions and cognitive cues of others. Think about it, have you ever passed a stranger and just got a sense that they were stressed or nervous? Well this is you making a quick emotional assumption on a complete stranger. Imagine actually having a full conversation with someone. As the focus on yourself changes, you start to adjust your R.A.S., your brain starts to find support automatically, without your effort. You then automatically behave in a confident way, and start to subtly put out a confident vibe. As this happens, you will start to notice changes in the way people react to you. You will start to pick up on people being more flirtatious and warm to you. People will pay more attention to you while being more accepting of your opinions and ideas. The beauty of this process is that even though we logically know that we're really just lying to ourselves, the brain is just designed to pick up on what's relevant and important. Just like the new car example, we start to notice positive elements about ourselves. We then start to feel more positive about ourselves, so we radiate confidence. This results in people starting to be friendlier to us, and acknowledging positive elements about ourselves. At that point you're in control of your own brain, rather than it controlling you.

This isn't just a process that turns you into a cocky narcissist. Rather, because you've been aware of the process while experiencing the benefits of it you can gain the most important evidence of all, which is that you never had a reason to not be confident with who you are. This is the evidence that a lot of people need in order to love themselves. Once you experience this effect, the process of being cocky or narcissistic is no longer needed as you start to actually understand your value. It's not enough for me to just tell you that you're ok just being you. Even with reading this now, it's not enough to just read "be confident, love yourself, blah blah blah". The brain needs new experienced evidence. This has to be something you experience for yourself. Neither I nor anyone else can tell you to "not be anxious, you have nothing to worry about". You need to gain the reference and evidence yourself. Once you start doing that, your brain starts to give you reasons to love yourself. This is how you go from just being cocky to genuinely confident.

THE POWER OF KNOWING

Genuine confidence comes from knowledge, whether that is from the evidence of positive self-concepts, or from knowledge about a subject you've studied, or a job you feel you're good at, for example. Knowledge brings about confidence. So just as you feel confident in something you know a lot about, confidence about yourself is no different. The more you know about yourself, the more confident you'll be. Now I'm not talking about an "in-the-moment" feeling of confidence like being stubborn or sure of something, but rather, an ease and comfort that you constantly feel in social environments. It's the ability to be congruent with who you are, regardless of the situation. You feel free to be the same way you are with your closest friends as you do with a stranger. This type of confidence comes from knowledge you acquire about yourself. But don't get caught in an "I know I'm not a confident guy" loop because that just goes nowhere.

Because self-concepts can be so abstract and difficult to define, as well as having our identities often change based on the situation, it can be difficult to pin point and know exactly who you are. So the best way to start knowing yourself is to be clear about what you want. The more clarity you have, the better. People who clearly know what they want tend to automatically create self-concepts that lead them towards those wants. They also automatically behave in ways that bring them closer to those wants. Everybody wants to have more money or wants to have their perfect mate but a lot of people don't know much past that. They aren't clear about how much money they want or what type of person they want in their life. Because these things aren't clearly defined, the brain doesn't bother to create the supporting self-concepts.

LIVING YOUR PURPOSE

The second strategy in this stage is called "Living Your Purpose". This is the process of living with intention. So there's the purpose itself, and then there's how to go about living it. I'll start with asking you "what's the purpose of your life?" If you can answer this question, great, if not then don't worry. People who know what they want in life radiate calmness and focus. They have a certainty about them that doesn't shake or waver when people question it. This is a confidence in what they want, and why they want it. Confidence comes when you make those decisions. People who know what their life's purpose is have those decisions made and have confidence in that. Here's the thing: most people can't answer the question of what their life's purpose is, so they never learn to develop the skill of intentionally living. This is why most people end up reacting to their environments, and coping through life, just dealing with what comes their way. Individuals who live with intention shape the world around them. They thrive through life and create their own environments instead of the environments creating them. It's the difference of being a rock or a leaf in the wind. But here's the good news, you don't need to answer the question of your life's purpose to start living with intention. You just need to make a decision about what you want in your life right now. Not for your whole life. But just for where you are right now, in the moment. This decision can change, so just pick something, anything. What do you have a passion or interest for right now? If your passion is art, make your purpose to touch the hearts and minds of the people who experience your art. If you're interested in science, make your purpose to be a constant learner and teacher of science. If you haven't found your passion yet, just decide on what you want right now. That could be being a sociable and confident person. It could be being the best student or worker you can be. If you can't decide on anything, make your purpose to just enjoy life to its fullest and soak in all it has to give you. All you need is a purpose, so make it anything; it doesn't have to be permanent. Once you make that decision, fuel it with reasons for why you want it. Think about what having this will do for your life. Think about how it will make you feel to have, or do, or be this purpose. The more reasons you have the better. The clearer you make this purpose and why you want it for yourself, the easier it is to live with intention. When this is done you'll also radiate a more confident you. So answer this these next questions.

Stop.
Think for a moment.
Be honest with yourself.
Then answer.

What do you want?

_____

Why do you want that?

_____

_____

_____

_____

What is your purpose?

_____

So you should have a "working" purpose now. I know by this stage I don't have to tell you to make sure you follow through, do I? But just in case you're reading this and you haven't answered the questions just asked. Stop reading now and go answer them. If you have, let me explain what I mean by how to "live" your purpose.

When I say Living with Purpose, what I mean is that your purpose fuels your behavior and emotional state. I'm not saying that everything you do has to be for your purpose. But just that you embrace your purpose as who you are and have certainty in the reasons it's your purpose. When you live with purpose, you disregard opinions that don't fuel that purpose. Not because you're being ignorant, but just because you're clear on the big picture of your wants, and are careful about the evidence you give your self concepts. Lets take a body builder for example. With a purpose to sculpt their body, they educate themselves on how to eat correctly, and train efficiently. Not only do they have the knowledge, but they are a living example of evidence for their knowledge. Imagine if someone who clearly hadn't stepped foot in a gym proceeded to tell him how to properly body build. The body builder would probably just laugh, and ignore the person. At no point would this person be valued as a source of evidence for the self-concept of being a knowledgeable body builder. This is what having certainty in your purpose does for you. It allows you to weed out negative influences and allows you to discredit people who don't know what they're talking about. You have to set your personal boundaries for what you will and won't allow in life. This ultimately comes from having clarity on what you want. Having your purpose allows you to clearly identify with something that you can have unshakeable confidence in.

PRE-DECIDING THE INTENTION

One of the ways you can apply this is by deciding ahead of time what your intentions are for upcoming days and experiences. When you do this, you apply the meaning to experiences beforehand. This is such a powerful tool in terms of developing new self-concepts and reducing anxiety and The Fear. Let me give you an example: have you ever had a day off work or school and as you went through that day you kept thinking about things you should or could be doing? Maybe you wandered around the house doing nothing, but feeling like you should be doing something. So you try to figure out if you should make food or just order in, you try to pick whichever way is quicker. But spend too much time just deciding so the whole process of picking was counter-productive. Then, as the feeling that "I should be productive" continues to grow, it develops into a feeling like "I'm wasting this day". Eventually, it becomes night, and you've given up. At this point you probably feel like shit because you did nothing with your day. Does any of this sound familiar? Well now try to remember the last relaxing day you had. Maybe you referred to it as your "lazy day". Again, you did nothing throughout your day. You wandered around the house, maybe made some food or ordered in. You were just lounging around, doing nothing all day. Well both days are the exact same. Nothing was done on either day. The only difference was the intention and purpose you had given to that day. The relaxing day was decided beforehand; it was your intention to do nothing that day. In return, your mind allowed you to relax, whereas the first example had you tossing around like a leaf in the wind as you struggled with thoughts of what you should be doing.

When you live your purpose, you preemptively decide the meaning and results of experiences. When you're clear on your purpose and why you're living it, you acquire clarity around how you interpret experiences. You can free yourself from outcomes and just be confident and comfortable knowing that you're being you and anyone who judges that, doesn't matter. As you push yourself to face your fears, decide the intention of the experience beforehand. Choose the meaning of the experience before your brain chooses for you. If you have approach anxiety with people you find attractive, and you're going to the bar with your friends, make it your intention to just get some reference experience so that you can get over The Fear. Your purpose may be to be a sociable person, so your intentions are just to remove your social anxiety. When this is clear, that's all the approaches mean to you. The experience just becomes references and new evidence, regardless of how the approaches panned out. You may meet some cool people or you might freeze up and look like a weirdo to a stranger. Regardless of the outcome, it's all just references. It's all just the process, and the little steps towards you getting over The Fear. When you pre-set your intention, you eliminate the possibility of negatively misinterpreting an experience. Ask yourself this: if you knew your purpose and why you wanted it, would you allow others to judge you on how you achieved it? Or imagine you had the perfect relationship. You find each other incredibly attractive and make each other extremely happy. If you want to be with your partner and your intentions are to spend your life with them, do you care if someone tells you they don't like your relationship, or that they don't find them attractive? I highly doubt it. Living your purpose also allows you to mentally step away from the sensations of The Fear. When experiencing The Fear becomes a choice you make yourself rather then being forced to face it, the sensation doesn't overwhelm you as much. This is because having the pre-determined intention tells your brain that its ok to experience this. So the experience of The Fear becomes justified because its just a step in the direction of your purpose, or better put, you're living your purpose. You can step away from things like embarrassment and rejection once you make up your own mind about the experiences beforehand.

CHALLENGE

So these are two strategies to reduce anxiety and build confidence. Adjusting your R.A.S. and Living Your Purpose. Start implementing them now, and take advantage of them as you push yourself through your fears. Before you move on to the next stage, please get in the habit of applying these strategies. Start picking out evidence, be narcissistic, be your biggest fan, every time you see your reflection point out what makes you sexy. Decide your purpose, and start living it. Make up your mind beforehand about how a situation will help your purpose. Continue the staring contest game, but if that isn't enough. Bump it up a notch and push yourself. Start giving random people compliments. Start asking basic questions or start conversations with people. If you're single, go out and get some numbers and set up some dates. You have to decide for yourself on how fast you want to get over The Fear and its anxiety. Just make sure you start to apply the strategies as you go along to help you. Thank you for your commitment this far. I wish you all the best in this journey.

STAGE 5

- You Vs. Others -

The Fear affects more than just who we are, it also affects our relationships with others. Not just romantic relationships, but our friendships too, by stifling our ability to relax. Fear makes it impossible to effectively communicate ourselves, or "who we are" to others. When you start experiencing the "in-the-moment response", your brain locks up, you can't think, you can't focus, and you certainly can't act like yourself. This stage will break down how anxiety influences our relationships. Teaching you how to be yourself with new friends or while approaching the "hot dish". As well as giving you tools on how to handle the anxiety while doing that.

MISATTRIBUTION THEORY

Psychologists have identified a particular flaw in how we naturally interpret anxiety. It's called the misattribution of arousal theory. The study that first identified this had a woman ask passing men to complete a quick survey for research. After they completed the survey, she would give them her number and tell them to call her if they had any questions about the research. After this happened, another person standing by would have the men rate how attracted they were to the woman giving the survey. This test was given on a street, on a sturdy bridge and on a very shaky and wobbly bridge. The results showed that the men found the woman most attractive when she surveyed them on the wobbly bridge. This theory has been repeatedly tested with different scenarios and genders. What it provided is an understanding about a fundamental error we make in how we understand our emotions. The misattribution theory explains that people have a problem differentiating anxiety from arousal and vice versa.

We misattribute excitement as nervousness and we confuse arousal as anxiety. This means that a lot of the time our brains have a problem understanding the difference between anxiety and excitement, or what to make of arousal. But if you think about it, the physical sensations are almost the same. Increased heart rate, increased sweating, inability to concentrate or sleep, butterflies in your stomach, etc. The only real difference is what's going on in our minds and how we perceive the situation. So for a lot of people they're just interpreting excitement as anxiety. The misattribution of arousal theory explains that when we feel any sort of heightened state, our minds leap towards possible causes. This ends up causing us to fear Ms. Legs-For-Days at the bar or the wanna-be-main-squeeze in class.

The Fear response is supposed to help us; it's actually your body's way of letting you know what's important. When you see someone attractive, your body uses this response as a way of telling you "hey, it's game time. Go over there and get 'em!" We are wired to look for traits to reproduce, so we gauge environments for the best possible mate. Our minds scan and search for attractive traits, not just physical ones but cognitive ones, like confidence and happiness. Once we spot these traits, the bell fires off and our body says "don't let this one go, you never know when you'll get another one". This is a product of our caveman times. We are wired for scarcity, because we didn't know when our next meal would be. We didn't know if we would live through the night, or be attacked by wild animals. We are wired to recognize value in everything from people, to financial opportunities. Our minds decide what's considered valuable in society, and our bodies prepare us to go get it. This is why a lot of people have problems being themselves around someone they find attractive. It's why you can easily talk and be yourself around someone you see as unattractive or just a friend. Ironically, however, because we want someone to like us and be with us, we filter who we are in hopes not to ruin our chances, not allowing ourselves to be liked. But behind the curtains of this effect there's a bunch of different things going on. Our bodies use arousal to prepare us, but because of the misattribution of arousal our minds confuse what that sensation means. We also have wiring to worry about our reputation. Mix rejection in there and you end up with a lot of us being conditioned to experience fear when faced with excitement. As we do this over and over, we start to interpret things like sexual tension as conflict, causing us to avoid experiences where attraction gets intense. So we need to recondition what anxiety means to us, so we can get back to having it help us.

You already know my philosophy on change, but once again, it's not enough for me to just tell you to know that your anxiety has just been excitement this whole time. You're going to have to have your own experiences to truly change. You do this by approaching a lot, every time you go out, by talking to strangers, starting conversations, giving compliments or asking questions, and by desensitizing The Fear and breaking down irrational anxieties. Like I have said before, The Fear response is always there, it's just what it means to you and how you react to it. If you've been following along with the challenges, you've already begun the process of re-tuning your anxiety with the staring contests. One of the most direct and intense ways to create tension with another person is though eye contact. Prolonged eye contact can be incredibly uncomfortable because it exposes who you are. It allows another person to gauge your intentions. You've probably even heard people refer to eyes as "the windows to your soul". This is because eye contact is used to express extreme intentions, whether that is to challenge someone or to be intimate with someone. Prolonged eye contact is used to express extreme aggression or attraction. When there's anger and aggression between two people there's a tension as they stare each other down. But when two people are incredibly attracted to each other and can't look away, there's a sexual tension. We have obviously been conditioned to avoid aggressive tension, but because a lot of us have been misattributing arousal we also become anxious with sexual tension. This is why I've been having you win the staring contests. As you do this you're slowly re-syncing the aggression vs attraction tensions, while allowing yourself to desensitize anxiety around eye contact.

THE TRUE PURPOSE OF ANXIETY

The Fear and your anxiety is supposed to help you indicate what's important. It's your indication to pursue and go after what your mind has decided has value to aid your survival and ability to reproduce. Now you don't have to actually want to reproduce with a person just because you find them attractive. But just know that this is what your body is trying to signal for you. Anxiety should be your indication that you should take action. Start reconditioning anxiety's meaning as just your cue to act.

Anxiety = Act

Now, obviously we know that some anxiety is caused by actual danger, like if a fight breaks out, that fear response kicks-starts your anxiety to get you to act, either by stopping it or avoiding it. But when it's just spotting the babe, then that's your cue to approach. When you first start doing approaches, everything will give you anxiety, even if you don't find them attractive. But with the more references and evidence you get, your anxiety and fear response will re-sync to its purpose.

THE NATURAL PATTERN OF REACTIONS

So let's look at the typical anxiety around approaching someone you find attractive. Most people will see the person, and then try to almost strategize the approach, deciding how to walk up and what to say. But as you've probably noticed, the longer you wait, the worse the anxiety gets. You end up psyching yourself out or buying into your excuses. Or maybe you try talking your way out of the anxiety. You start telling yourself you shouldn't be feeling it, or that there is no reason to be anxious. As you know, this only makes it worse. This is because there is a natural pattern to our reactions. It goes Attention, Emotions, Actions. Your attention activates your emotions and your emotions influence your actions; those new actions change your attention and so on. When you try to talk yourself out of anxiety you're just fighting against the natural process. It's you placing attention to your anxiety, getting more anxious emotions, then not taking action because you psyched yourself out. You want to work with the natural flow of this pattern. If you're feeling anxiety don't go against it by placing more attention to it. Change your actions. The sooner you change your actions the sooner your attention will change. You can use this to your advantage by forcing behavior that takes your attention away from the anxiety. You probably remember what to do if you catch fire, right?

Stop, drop and roll.

Well this is a cheesy application of this motto, but it works. Stop your attention, Drop the emotion, and Roll with the behavior. Stop the over-thinking, and just acknowledge the anxiety as being there. Understand its purpose and drop your attention on it, then act on that purpose of that anxiety. Embrace the flow of this pattern.

Change your focus.

As you feel anxious, your thoughts will go all over the place. You can stop these thoughts by interrupting your thinking with something completely different or random. Just like a person with ADHD who quickly shifts topics, pick a new one. Another way is to become aware of how you're being affected. You can do this by taking note of your breathing, heart rate or any other physical change. As you do this, you can become aware of the sensation as a separate thing from you.

Recognize the sensation as one thing, and yourself as the subject of this sensation as another.

It's an in-the-moment awareness of "who" is interpreting the sensation. If The Fear, biological response is too intense for you, burn some of it off by flexing and stretching yourself out. You have a lot of adrenaline in your system when you're anxious.

Tense your muscles and body for as long as you can.

Have a pre-planned distraction that you're going to use to control your focus like a change in your behavior. Even if that behavior is to start humming a song in your head or to jump around, do whatever you need to do to distract yourself and complete the approach. Even if you embarrass yourself or totally freeze up, you still completed the approach. If starting up a conversation is too intense, just as we explained in Stage 3, break down the steps. Start by just approaching to say "hi," and then "bye", and walk away. Sure, it's a little weird, but who cares. You know why you're doing this and that's all that matters. You want to be able to develop the skill to effectively communicate yourself in any moment, because this isn't something that's going to fix itself, it requires desensitization and the ability to be comfortable with The Fear. Remember, the point is to just get references and evidence that eliminate your social anxiety. You don't need to date the person, or have sex with the person. Your mind set should be, "I'm just having fun socializing and living my purpose".   Don't see this as you getting something from the other person, like sex, or a phone number. It's just two people getting to know each other, that's it. You're going to get a lot of rejection too, and that's completely fine, but we'll talk more about that in the next stage.

You'll find that as you start doing approaches, and once you start having the conversation, your anxiety drops dramatically and instantly. However, you'll still feel The Fear response preparing your body. This is because approach anxiety and the fears around it are made up in your head. As you get familiar with having conversations with new people, you can start to relax and become more like yourself. Being able to meet new people and accurately portray yourself is an essential part of life. Firstly, it allows you to find people that you're compatible with. Secondly, it allows you to be yourself right from the start of meeting someone. A lot of the time, when we feel anxious we have a tendency to just agree with people for the sake of avoiding more tension. Or lying about something because we don't want to draw attention to ourselves. The problem is that if you're trying to get to know someone for the first time you're giving a dishonest representation of who you are. A lot of people believe that they won't be accepted or liked if they act like themselves.

I've found that people are rarely upset with who a person is. Rather, people get upset when you break the expectations of who you perceived yourself to be.

This is why being yourself from the start is so important.

CHALLENGE

So with that said, I want you to up your game, wherever you are at in your journey. Bump up the intensity, and start to create challenges for yourself that really start to freak you out. Go ask that fit bird for her number or out on a date. Go start a conversation with a stranger. Go make some new friends. Get yourself in the face of fear and learn to act the moment your anxiety indicates. Apply the techniques to help ease The Fear, but make sure you complete your challenges. You need to get in the habit of being comfortable with discomfort. Again only you can demand this of yourself. I want to give you the right tools for the job but you have to do your part. So get out there, step it up and challenge yourself.

STAGE 6

- You Vs. Society -

Stage 6 will address a core root around anxiety and its effect on your relationship with society. The topic of this stage will be about rejection, or more specifically the fear of rejection. While there can be many reasons for why someone feels like they shouldn't put themselves out in the world, the fear of rejection is usually at the base of all of them. Not only do most people carry this worry, but it also warps people's perception of the world and society. When breaking down the fear of rejection there are two elements. There's the issue of actually dealing with rejection and then there is the act of trying to avoid rejection. This stage will focus on both of these elements and teach you how to handle rejection like a pro.

What makes rejection so brutal to handle at first is how it can feel like your entirety is being rejected, rather than just something you did or shared. Imagine sharing your passion with people, like music you've written or some art you've created and having it receive negative feedback. Well it's common in these experiences to feel as though you yourself were rejected, rather than just your art. A lot of this has to do with the passion and love we put into our creativity, but once again, it's those self-concepts and identity coming into play. Let's take another example of opening up to someone about how you feel and not having them feel the same or even just being rejected to go on a date. We often attribute these experiences as "all of us being rejected", instead of the situation not being right or just a lack of immediate chemistry. Any rejection feels like a personal attack on us, rather than the situation at hand. Rejection to us feels like we aren't worthy or "enough" to get or give love.

The fear of rejection keeps us from putting ourselves in socially-exposing situations as well. But regardless of this, life often forces us to go out of our comfort zone once in-a-while, making those socially-exposing situations become impossible to avoid. So how do we process rejection when we can't dodge it? Our brains attach a meaning to the rejection in order to process it. And based on those self-concepts we talked about earlier, the meaning comes from how our lens of ourselves views the world. The meaning that becomes attached is always an explanation to the behavior. It's an assumption about the motivations behind an action. Take a confident person for example: they would interpret the experience of being denied a date as "That's a shame, but if they don't want to get to know me, oh well, no worries, their loss". So the explanation behind the behavior of rejection would be "They're probably just interested in someone else or I am not their personal physical taste, or maybe they're just focused on other things in life other than relationships. Regardless, no worries". Whenever we talk about evidence to support a self-concept there is always an explanation or assumption about why the experience happened the way it did. But the explanation is made up by the self-concept. However, all that can be known is that the "act" of one person denying another person of a date happened. Us as interpreters have to perceive the act, and place an explanation to the act. These explanations are just assumptions; they're just self-drawn conclusions about the act.

EGO PROTECTION

Because our identities, emotions and egos are involved, we are slightly inclined to perceive things in whatever favors feeling less pain or more pleasure. This means protecting our ego, confidence and self-worth, as well. I'm sure you've had the experience of being caught up in a fight with a significant other or friend at some point in your life. Well, have you ever found that somewhere along the fight you forgot about the actual reason you were fighting. All you knew was that you had to win or get the last word in. If this sounds familiar to you then you've experienced this effect of ego protection. This need to protect the ego from rejection and the pain it can bring is a massive component to why a lot of people won't put themselves out there. But without getting anymore in-depth with the psychology of the ego, let's look at how rejection alters our perception of society.

INSECURITIES

Now, this ego protection really messes with our ability to handle rejection. Because of this, there are ramifications to our perceptions.

This is because the inability to handle rejection creates insecurities. When we can't face a harsh reality of something, we make assumptions and explanations that protect our ego.

This isn't necessarily a bad thing. But my point in explaining this is that it can create some negative and misconstrued ideas about society that don't serve you in the long run. An example of this would be a guy who approaches the babe at the club. Say the girl wasn't having it and gets weirded out and ignores the guy. The person then makes the assumption that this girl is just a bitch, and continues on socializing. On the one hand the guy didn't allow for the negative experience to mess with his self-concept or mood. But if this guy keeps getting this result when approaching women, this assumption makes it impossible to realize that he needs to take a different approach or improve his social skills. It's a double-edged sword; this is why the topic of rejection is being explained this late into the program. There is an order to development and understanding. Just as you don't need to find a body sculptor if you're overweight, you just need to start doing anything active. You don't need to worry about how to get better socially until you start getting over your fears of being socially vulnerable. But because of this ego protection we have an inclination to avoid error and failure and try to do things perfect the first time around. Progress isn't made that way; it's made with consistent effort and exposure, which means trial and error.

These assumptions that protect our egos create insecurities. Our insecurities are the long-term product of not being able to handle rejection, just as confidence is the long-term product of facing your fears.

FANTASY

As we continue to make assumptions, they accumulate into our beliefs about the world. Just as we learned before, the brain fills in its own evidence to support ideas. This results in what I call having a Fantasy-Based Perception. It's an idea about the nature of society and how it works. But this perception is not supported by actual experienced evidence, but rather by cultural standards such as media and religion. Living in a fantasy-based perception gives you inaccurate emotions that result in negative and insecure behavior. This is because fantasy-based perceptions are delusional. It's based on what you think is out there, rather than actual evidence. So let's take movies and music, a lot of the time they are usually adaptations of what love is. This results in a belief about how love should be or come about. This is how a fantasy-based perception can have its effect on your beliefs. It has you believing that the perfect person will just stumble into your life without you doing anything. This person will make all the moves and simultaneously be able to see through any insecurities or social anxieties you have, seeing only the true and best version of you. Well, this, my friend, is wishful, delusional thinking that supports you not having to do anything but wait. These fantasy-based perceptions can also portray ideas like love at first sight, or the notion of soul mates. But the reality of the matter is that people usually just end up with who's in their proximities. There are definitely examples of having two strangers who meet at a coffee shop randomly and hit it off. But this relies on both people being able to effectively communicate themselves, as well as having the same immediate relationship wants and a massive amount of other variables. Accepting the reality of this can be hard, because it means that yes, you will have to face your fears, and yes you will have to deal with rejection. But I promise you, reality-based perceptions are much more rewarding. They give you control of your life. They give you the motivation to go out and make life happen instead of being at the will of waiting for things to change in life. On top of this, fantasy-based perceptions can give you incorrect emotional reactions and behaviors that do more harm than good.

LOVE AT FIRST SIGHT

Have you ever found yourself falling in love or having romantic emotions towards someone who's new to work or school that you've just met or talked to once? Or maybe you've seen a friend or someone you know who's experienced this. They go on and on about someone they don't know, saying things like "Ah, they're just so beautiful and smart and nice. I think this is love. This is crazy, we haven't talked yet but, ugh, this must be love". While fun to watch or roll your eyes at (maybe this isn't your first rodeo), chances are if they went and shared how they felt, your friend probably creeped their crush out and was met with rejection. If you can relate to this or have seen this before let me explain what's really going on. It's one thing to find someone attractive and something completely different to think you know someone to the point where you have romantic feelings about them. The fantasy-based perception had your friend feeling those emotions because of an idea of how to experience love. Those ideas create assumptions and explanations around how to understand the feeling of being attracted to someone. The fantasy-based perception attributes an understanding about a person without any actual evidence of spending time with them or getting to know them. For the sake of explanation, let's assume this is you going through this falling-in-love without evidence business. Here's the harsh reality around what's really going on with this experience. As you feel physically attracted, your mind needs to make sense as to why, that's when the fantasy-based perception clicks in and fills in the gaps to make sense of the emotion. Once the gaps are filled with false assumptions and misunderstood attractions, you get welled-up with "love" and decide to tell them how you feel. This is seen as you pushing your false perception of the person onto them, and that is almost always met with resistance.

When your mind is forced to fill a gap about who a person is, the assumptions often come from their appearance and what you expect from someone who looks like that.

You maybe attribute personality traits like kindness or intelligence to the person, but because they aren't grounded in facts or evidence from actually getting to know them, it's really you just telling them who they should be. The idea of "who they are" comes from incorrect assumptions fed to you by culture as well as poor interpretations of past experiences. Think about it, haven't you ever made a quick judgement about someone just based on how they look? Assuming someone was an asshole or a bitch just because of their appearance or the clothing brand they wore, only to find out later they were really sweet? This is the fantasy-based perception making assumptions and false conclusions.

THE EXPECTATION AROUND WORDS

But the real problem is not that you think someone is really kind or smart, but rather how your mind interprets those words when there isn't any backing evidence. The mind takes the epitome and total essence of traits like "kindness" and "intelligence" and attributes them to the person, making you believe you know their true selves. This makes you feel like you love them, as well as seeing the essence of who they really are, when in actuality you're just perceiving the person as your interpretation of what pure "kindness" or pure "intelligence" is to you. So when you're all welled-up with this feeling of love and passion for someone you haven't really gotten to know, then decide to express how you feel, it can really creep them out. Now it's not my intention for this to sound mean, and maybe this isn't the case in your experience, but my point is to try and give you an understanding and awareness about the behind-the-scenes of this experience. Look at behavior found in romantic movies, for example. A lot of it appears romantic because of the grand gestures shown and the impulsivity and intensity of the whole thing. But story tellers have about two hours to wrap up an entire relationship, so we can't see the hours of conversation, we just see highlights. So if you step back and really think about if that behavior were to happen in real life, a lot of it would come off stalker-like or just plain creepy. We are given massively skewed ideas about how to understand and experience emotions like passion and love. Unfortunately, the experiences that these notions lead us towards can create a lot more confusion than clarity. After just a few bad experiences, you can really start to provide your own evidence for a negative belief about people or the world. This is that ego protection kicking in to make sense of the behaviors of rejection so you don't have to face the reality that you creeped them out. It's fantasy-based perceptions that have you placing people on pedestals, attributing them with unachievable standards like being the essence of kindness or intelligence. What you're doing is attributing perfection to a perception of a person.

THE HONEYMOON PHASE

The fantasy-based perception is the reason that a lot of people fall in love with a person just because of how they look, without actually getting to know them. It's also an explanation to the honeymoon phase new couples go through. Two people hit it off, after spending a while "waiting for love". Through the excitement of the initial attraction, they each attribute the other person as the essence of whatever positive concept they think they are. They then start dating and finally start to see the reality of who the other person is, and how maybe they aren't the essence of kindness during that first fight. Then the "fantasy" or honeymoon phase starts to slip away. Fantasy-based perceptions break down with actual evidence. As you start to question why you feel the way you feel, you start to see just how much this affects your interpretation of the world. The problem is that it's hard to accept that you do not perceive the world accurately, because that usually means taking a shot or two to your ego. Fantasy is addictive because it protects your insecurities. It also usually justifies and supports not taking action to fix them. Just as mentioned before, you might see someone you assume is a douche or a bitch and avoid approaching them because of this assumption when in fact it doesn't have any actual grounding.

HYPER SENSITIVITY

Another way fantasy-based perceptions affect you is by giving you a heightened sensitivity to social exposure. What this means is that you make assumptions about very little details that more often than not don't mean anything. An example of this would be you posting a photo on Instagram and starting to make assumptions about people liking it or not. You start thinking a particular person "liked" your photo to communicate interest in you. When in actuality they may have just been bored online and liking everyone's photos. Fantasy-based perceptions can have you placing extreme amounts of importance to small things. Like you assuming a person will know you like them if you "like" an old photo of them. Or you thinking that people notice every detail of your appearance or hair if it's an off-day.

You are your own worst critic.

People don't care as much as we think they do. You probably don't think much of other people's appearance unless it's being compared to yours. Your confidence shouldn't change based on what you wear. But yet a large majority of people are like this. Everyone feels as though their actions and words are going to be extremely judged. But just as you don't think much of a person if they ask a question in class or a meeting, people don't think much of you for speaking up. People being indifferent or not liking a painting you made is not a rejection of you. It's just a small opinion with a bunch of influencing variables unrelated to you that didn't result in your favor. This is all rejection is. It's just you making a big deal out of the little self-concepts of others.

The goal is not to avoid experiencing rejection forever as our ego has tried to make happen, but rather to be desensitized to it. It's to lose the hyper-sensitivity to criticism and to just relax with being ourselves. It's ok for everyone not to like you or your passions. It's supposed to be this way. You're not supposed to be able to just fall in love with anybody and have everybody fall in love with you.

You're supposed to have preferences and want different things than other people. This is what makes life interesting: being able to enjoy the differences.

The goal is to be able to effectively share and communicate these preferences with other people. So when you do come across other people you're actually similar with, it means more, because this way it's grounded in evidence of actually knowing another person and not just a fantasy.

BREAKING DOWN FANTASY

So instead of trying to crack down on every single fantasy-based perception, we want to look back at the fundamentals of its cause - again, attacking the roots of the problem, just as we explained earlier. Fantasy-based perceptions are the result of our insecurities around being rejected. Because rejection is inevitable, we might as well get used to it. The way we do this is by going against our ego's protection system. In order to get over rejection we need to get used to being rejected and judged. We desensitize ourselves to it by experiencing it repeatedly. Here's the thing, a lot of people preach the "not giving a fuck" mentality. Well, there is a massive difference between "not giving a fuck" and actual self-acceptance. Actual self-acceptance comes from becoming comfortable with rejection, seeing it as a natural part of society. Actual self-acceptance and confidence comes from evidence and experience that was earned. A large majority of people who claim to "not to give a fuck" actually give tons of "fucks". They're really just strengthening their fantasy-based perceptions to a point where they can no longer relate to other people. Sure, this inability to relate makes it easier to not care about people. But doing this is robbing yourself of the joys of genuinely enjoying another person's depth. You can tell who is like this because they have a hyper-sensitivity to exposure. They take massive offense to criticism and they become hostile when people don't like them.

People with actual self-acceptance and confidence enjoy criticism, and find humor in their flaws. They don't take things too seriously and are comfortable with people not liking them.

These people can actually produce results and actually know what they're capable of because they have the evidence to prove it. This difference is also the difference between cockiness and confidence. People who are cocky think they could actually seduce any person they want. They think they could make music or art that all people enjoy, but they don't have the experience or evidence to back this up, so they just make excuses instead. This is why actually desensitizing yourself to rejection and becoming comfortable with it is essential to actual confidence.

BACK TO REALITY

There is no better way to become comfortable with rejection then embarrassment. When you force yourself to be embarrassed, you start to see how little people concern themselves with your life. You start to become comfortable with making mistakes and having failures. You start to break down your insecurities by providing evidence of surviving by just being you. Your fantasy-based perceptions also change into reality based ones as you can now go out and experience more differences in people. The sensation of forcing embarrassment is also a lot different than accidentally embarrassing yourself. You can control the variables so that you don't have the ramifications of embarrassing yourself when it counts. This is done by doing these exercises with complete strangers outside of your social circle and normal environment. Start with being as anonymous as you can be, if possible. It's a good entry into this process.

CHALLENGE

Go to a busy street or mall across town and walk up to strangers and make a crazy request like, "Hey, can you twist my nipple please", or "Hey, could you pat my head please". Most people will respond with something like, "Sorry, what did you just say", or "Umm, sure . . ." Just ask them again or thank them anyways and go to a new person. Worst case scenario, you gave them something to talk about over dinner that night. If this is too much for you, again, baby step it. Start by just walking up to a person and saying "hi", then wait an awkward 10 seconds and say "bye" and walk away. If approaching strangers is too much, wear a ridiculous hat in public or something that embarrasses you. If you want to get really crazy, go up to people and ask for a kiss. This process is a lot like approach anxiety that we talked about yesterday except actively choosing to bomb an approach. Once that anxiety around approaching is gone you need to work on being ok with being embarrassed and being comfortable with rejection. Doing this will skyrocket your results and also help you in other areas of life as you start to re-tune your perception and emotions to reality. So have fun with this. Do what amuses you. If you think something is weird and funny, do it to amuse yourself. Get in the habit of self-amusement. As you get comfortable with this, you'll find it very easy to be yourself around new people. Progress happens quickly and the results are empowering and addictive. So enjoy yourself, have some fun, and good luck.

STAGE 7

- The Final Points -

We don't have to consciously think about how to drive a car, or get to and from work. It's just a mindless process we do without thinking. The majority of our day is spent in this state, because being in a constant stage of self-awareness would be exhausting and overwhelming. Our psychological homeostasis forces us to go on auto-pilot to reserve energy. This is the automatic setting touched on earlier. We aren't designed to actively be aware of every action we take. Like looking at the door knob and putting our hand to it, turning it, and then pulling the door open. Being this way slows us down and uses mental effort that could be applied to other, more important things. It might sound silly but the effort of mental awareness and thinking is one of the hardest jobs to do. There's a good chance that once you get familiar with your job you can do it on auto-pilot, right? So the fact of the matter is that we spend most of our time on auto-pilot with moments of awareness that break up our day into segments. This auto-pilot turns off when emotionally-relevant experiences happen. This means, when shit hits the fan, you become aware so that you can handle the situation. But as we know, the more you experience The Fear, the more it desensitizes. So the more desensitized you become with anxiety and fear, the easier it becomes to be yourself on auto-pilot. But here's the thing, even though you're aware, you will still rely on the pilot to take over.

You will respond with the patterns and behaviors that are most familiar to you.

This is why we do things like fire drills in school and work. Repetition of a response is the best way to replicate the behavior, regardless of the emotion at hand.

PUBLIC SPEAKING

So when it comes to things like public speaking, it's time to train the pilot. Successful public speaking comes down to repetition, this may seem obvious, but it's essential. The more familiar you are with your speech, the easier it is to repeat it automatically without letting stage fright or The Fear affect you. If possible, go to the location where you're speaking and rehearse there, or practice beforehand. The more familiar you are with your speech, the better. This way, once you get up on stage you can let your pilot drive while you focus on reducing your anxiety and responding to the crowd. The best public speakers can speak from their heart and with the passion of their topic. They know how to explain their topic in many ways and just focus on what needs to be said verses a mindless memorization of the words. But for beginners, just focus on memorization and repetition. The better prepared you are in advance, the more natural your speech will appear, and the less nervous you will be.

Another way to make yourself comfortable before a public speech is to socialize with the audience, go introduce yourself to people you don't know. Become familiar with people so it's not just strangers you're speaking to. As you start to speak, notice your body, keep a confident and comfortable posture, stretch out, and move around, if you need. Make eye contact with the people you know in the audience. Breathe nice, slow breaths and take your time. Once you start, you'll instantly feel less anxious. If you have a podium in front of you hold onto it as you start, let it anchor you and keep you still if your hands or legs are shaking. Keep your focus on the content, and reading the vibe of the audience. Remember that The Fear is just an automatic response, and that this is supposed to be fun. So embrace the feelings and enjoy yourself. As you practice and repeat the content, the pilot turns into more of roller coaster attendant. In which you just get on the ride, hold on, enjoy, and get off. Public speaking becomes less like flying a plane and more like going along a set track. There is a ton of information out there on how to become an excellent public speaker that's worth looking up, but for now, the focus is on the anxiety.

ALTERNATIVES

When designing The Fear, I kept the focus on psychological strategies and tools to produce results. It's impossible to fully get over anxiety without the mental backing of experience. There are no drugs on the market that will eradicate anxiety or fear. Sure you can reduce the sensations with medication, but this is really just robbing you from the juiciness of conquering them yourself. But for people that are only interested in a temporary fix for a particular public speaking event, it can be worthwhile to look into diets and natural supplements to reduce anxiety beforehand.

HAPPINESS

The last topic I want to bring up is happiness. While the question of "what is happiness?" is complex and very subjective, there have been some fantastic philosophers on the subject that have shed some light on the topic. But what I want to explore is some common similarities in the way we all experience happiness. The experience of happiness can be broken down into two types. There is "Now-happiness" and "After-happiness".

Now-happiness refers to "in-the-moment" happiness. This is you feeling emotions of joy, ecstasy, and relaxation. These are experiences in which you aren't thinking, or having thoughts bombard you. It's loosing yourself to the environment and going wherever it takes you. This type of happiness is a lot like really immersive sex, being out with friends, or being completely relaxed on vacation. This type of happiness can only be experienced in the moment you're living it, unlike After-happiness.

After-happiness is a reflective happiness, it's you experiencing happiness when reminiscing on life. This experience of happiness is you thinking about the "old days" or laughing about what you've been through in your past. Like sitting in your rocking chair as an old person and remembering previous experiences. After-happiness is you recreating past events with a new perspective on life.

Remember that the topic is happiness. There are a lot of things we can reminisce about that bring up sorrow, anger, or even longing. However there is a clear difference about what evicts happiness or laughter while reminiscing. After-happiness often involves remembering stressful, anxious, or even embarrassing moments, and laughing about them in the present. You've probably heard the saying, "time heals all things". Well, a lot of that has to do with the fact that when we review our embarrassing or anxious moments with a new perspective, we can laugh about ourselves or feel good about the fact that we did have that experience. Think about embarrassing moments like bombing a speech, or freezing up when you talked to a childhood crush. You can probably laugh about the experience now. Sure, it may have caused a lot of pain or discomfort back then, but now, when the experience is no longer relevant, you have a story to laugh about. After-happiness is caused when you look back at moments where you pushed yourself, such as facing fears, or crazy and embarrassing things you've done in the process. The funny thing about After-happiness memories is that you were most likely in your head during those moments, freaking out, over-thinking, and just plain stressing out. But looking back on those times you can be proud and happy that you experienced those challenges.

The odd thing about reminiscing is that it almost reverses a lot of your emotions. When you think about embarrassing moments you can laugh about them now. When you think of painful ones you can feel pride about getting over them. But then you think about Now-happiness moments you feel sadness or longing because you wish you could feel that now.

Let's take a person who wants to get their ideal body, but they still don't have it. When they reminisce on moments where they indulged in junk food or skipped the gym to sleep-in, they have regret and wish that they had stayed disciplined. But in the moment of those decisions it felt pretty good downing that fast food or hitting the snooze button. Now-happiness moments often make you feel bad when reminiscing, either because of longing or because of regret. But let's take a person who has their ideal body, when they look back at the pain and struggle of working out and keeping disciplined they feel pride and happiness about having pushed through.

In the future, you're going to laugh about how nervous you got, or how silly it was to be this anxious over talking to the cutie. You will look back at pushing yourself through these challenges and feel a sense of pride. Plus you'll find the crazy stories you have quite entertaining.

Your anxieties now will be your amusements later.

You will actually get to a point where you miss getting as anxious as you do now. Because when you look back, your emotions were so intense going through these experiences. I'm not saying don't get over your anxieties, but rather there is a happiness in discomfort.

I'm sure you can guess by now how happiness relates to getting over your anxieties. The best way to improve the amount of happiness you feel about your life is to consistently challenge and push yourself. The more comfortable you get with discomfort, the more happiness you will feel looking back at your life, firstly, because of feeling the After happiness about your efforts, and secondly, because as you start to understand this, you start to associate positive feelings in the moments that you feel anxiety, just as people start to love working out. First the burn was painful and uncomfortable, and then after a while, they can't get enough of it. Humans are notorious for finding ways to enjoy the perversions of pain. We can be addicted to anything. Once you get addicted to the high of pushing past your fears and constantly challenging and developing into the best version of yourself, you won't be able to stop.

The effort you put in now you get to keep, and the effort you fail to give will haunt you.

Take the challenge to master your social inhibitions as the first step to creating an extraordinary life. Then keep the momentum up, don't let your high school or college years be your best years in life. If you feel that you're not living in the best time of your life, then that should be your cue that it's time for change. Regardless of your personality type, whether introverted or extroverted, we all need people; we are social creatures. The sooner you embrace that, the quicker you'll enjoy the greatest pleasures life has to offer. Financial achievement and health goals can bring you happiness, but if you don't have anyone to share it with, they're pointless. The pleasure of having a fantastic relationship with another person can extinguish the need for anything else in life. The more you share your gifts and passions with the world the more the world gives back. Be an individual who creates and gives rather then takes and judges. We all know it's better to give than to receive. The excitement you get from giving a gift you're proud of feels better than actually receiving presents, just as being able to share your ideas and humor with the world feels better than trying to just be entertained by others.

Memories are always made when emotions are high, good or bad. Just like not remembering the shirt you were wearing three Thanksgivings ago, but remembering your first love or first heartbreak. Allow yourself to experience the highs and lows of conquering over your anxiety. You have this one life, and you owe it to yourself to get the most out of it. This is what I want for you, and this is the reason I want to help you get over your social fears in life. The social element in life and the memories we make with others are what's most memorable. They have the ability to destroy us or empower us to heights of pleasure that aren't obtainable alone. The connections and friendships you make are what you get to keep when you look back at your life. The quality of your life will be a direct relationship to the amount of effort you give to it. Go out and demand this of yourself. Don't spend your life in the vortex of social media and living vicariously through other people, aimlessly distracted, mindlessly scrolling and watching hours of content that only keep your focus away from the problems in your life. This is life, right now, as you're reading this. Make a commitment to yourself to get the most out of it. Start by never rejecting an invite to go out, regardless of the people or situation. Allow yourself to indulge the endless possibilities of new experiences. Make new friends, and try new things. Take it all in! Surrender to the night and just enjoy the ride. Sure, a night in, relaxing and doing nothing can be refreshing but forcing yourself to make plans or to commit to volunteering or doing things with others is where memories are made. I promise you, you will not remember the endless hours of time you spent on your computer or phone. You will not remember the fun you had binge watching a television series alone on Netflix. So do this for yourself. Thank you for letting me share the strategies that have helped me, and have changed my own life. I wish you all the best, my friend.

Notes:

Proof

Made in the USA
Charleston, SC
17 June 2015